British History in Perspective
General Editor: Jeremy Black

00062626

PUBLISHED TITLES

Rodney Barker *Politics, Peoples and Government*
C. J. Bartlett *British Foreign Policy in the Twentieth Century*
Jeremy Black *Robert Walpole and the Nature of Politics
in Early Eighteenth-Century Britain*
Anne Curry *The Hundred Years War*
John W. Derry *British Politics in the Age of Fox, Pitt and Liverpool*
William Gibson *Church, State and Society, 1760–1850*
Ann Hughes *The Causes of the English Civil War*
Ronald Hutton *The British Republic, 1649–1660*
Kevin Jefferys *The Labour Party since 1945*
D. M. Loades *The Mid-Tudor Crisis,1545–1565*
Diarmaid MacCulloch *The Later Reformation in England, 1547–1603*
Keith Perry *British Politics and the American Revolution*
A. J. Pollard *The Wars of the Roses*
David Powell *British Politics and the Labour Question, 1868–1990*
Michael Prestwich *English Politics in the Thirteenth Century*
Richard Rex *Henry VIII and the English Reformation*
G. R. Searle *The Liberal Party: Triumph and Disintegration, 1886–1929*
Paul Seaward *The Restoration, 1660–1668*
Robert Stewart *Party and Politics, 1830–1852*
John W. Young *Britain and European Unity, 1945–92*

History of Ireland

D. G. Boyce *The Irish Question and British Politics, 1868–1986*

History of Scotland

Keith M. Brown *Kingdom or Province? Scotland and the Regal Union,
1603–1715*

History of Wales

J. Gwynfor Jones *Early Modern Wales, c.1525–1640*

Please see overleaf for forthcoming titles

D1078547

FORTHCOMING TITLES

Peter Catterall *The Labour Party, 1918–1940*
Eveline Cruickshanks *The Glorious Revolution*
John Davis *British Politics, 1885–1931*
David Dean *Parliament and Politics in Elizabethan and
Jacobean England, 1558–1614*
Susan Doran *English Foreign Policy in the Sixteenth Century*
David Eastwood *England, 1750–1850: Government and Community
in the Provinces*
Colin Eldridge *The Victorians Overseas*
Brian Golding *The Normans in England 1066–1100:
Conquest and Colonisation*
Steven Gunn *Early Tudor Government, 1485–1558*
Richard Harding *The Navy, 1504–1815*
Angus Hawkins *British Party Politics, 1852–1886*
H. S. Jones *Political Thought in Nineteenth Century Britain*
Anthony Milton *Church and Religion in England, 1603–1642*
R. C. Nash *English Foreign Trade and the World Economy, 1600–1800*
W. M. Ormrod *Political Life in England, 1300–1450*
Richard Ovendale *Anglo-American Relations in the Twentieth Century*
David Powell *The Edwardian Crisis: Britain, 1901–1914*
Brian Quintrell *Government and Politics in Early Stuart England*
Alan Sykes *The Radical Right in Britain*
Ann Williams *Kingship and Government in Pre-Conquest England*
Michael Young *Charles I*

History of Ireland

Sean Duffy *Ireland in the Middle Ages*
Hiram Morgan *Ireland in the Early Modern Periphery, 1534–1690*
Toby Barnard *The Kingdom of Ireland, 1641–1740*
Alan Heesom *The Anglo-Irish Union, 1800–1922*

History of Scotland

Bruce Webster *Scotland in the Middle Ages*
Roger Mason *Kingship and Tyranny? Scotland 1513–1603*
John Shaw *The Political History of Eighteenth Century Scotland*
John McCaffrey *Scotland in the Nineteenth Century*
I. G. C. Hutchinson *Scottish Politics in the Twentieth Century*

History of Wales

A. D. Carr *Medieval Wales*
Gareth Jones *Wales, 1700–1980: Crisis of Identity*

Please also note that a sister series, *Social History in Perspective*, is now available, covering the key topics in social, cultural and religious history.

THE LATER REFORMATION IN ENGLAND 1547–1603

Diarmaid MacCulloch

MACMILLAN

© Diarmaid MacCulloch 1990

All rights reserved. No reproduction, copy or transmission of this publication may be made without written permission.

No paragraph of this publication may be reproduced, copied or transmitted save with written permission or in accordance with the provisions of the Copyright, Designs and Patents Act 1988, or under the terms of any licence permitting limited copying issued by the Copyright Licensing Agency, 90 Tottenham Court Road, London W1P 9HE.

Any person who does any unauthorised act in relation to this publication may be liable to criminal prosecution and civil claims for damages.

First published 1990 by
MACMILLAN PRESS LTD
Houndmills, Basingstoke, Hampshire RG21 2XS
and London
Companies and representatives
throughout the world

ISBN 0–333–41928–6 hardcover
ISBN 0–333–41929–4 paperback

A catalogue record for this book is available
from the British Library.

11 10 9 8 7 6 5 4 3
03 02 01 00 99 98 97 96 95

Printed in Hong Kong

CONTENTS

Contents

For Nigel and Jennie MacCulloch

PREFACE

This little book makes no pretensions to originality; if it helps
to give a picture of how recent research has opened up our
understanding of the later Tudor Church, it will have
achieved its aim. I am grateful to have been part of the
company of scholars who have engaged in this exploration,
and, in particular to Professor Sir Geoffrey Elton, whose
friendship and guidance I can never sufficiently repay. I
must thank the following for their kindness in allowing me to
use their unpublished work: Eugene Bourgeois, Margaret
Clark, Ronald Fritze, David Peet, Robert Whiting. Professor
Patrick Collinson offered me some extremely helpful com-
ments on the text. I can additionally acknowledge the
helpfulness and efficiency of Macmillan, and, in particular,
of Vanessa Graham. Once more my colleagues and students
at Wesley College, Bristol, and in the University of Bristol
have given more than they realised towards my thoughts.
Mark Achurch deserves my especial gratitude for putting up
with the writing of this book.

Readers looking for the biases which still inevitably lie
behind the writing of religious history should note that I am
an ordained clergyman of the Church of England. In view of
the current growth of an unthinking conservatism and
insularity within that Church, I am indebted to my parents
for showing me in my childhood what the thoughtful and
tolerant face of Anglicanism can be. It is with loving thanks

for all that they have done for me that I return them the small present of this book.

DIARMAID MacCULLOCH

Wesley College, Bristol

1

SETTING THE SCENE

However destructive or dangerous in life, longlived and powerful monarchs often succeed in dying amid their subjects' grief; this seems as true of Henry VIII as it was of Josef Stalin. Across Henry's realm, public mourning penetrated the most remote places in January and February 1547, revealed to us for instance in numerous churchwardens' payments for funeral peals commemorating the dead King. Yet in the city of London, the ceremonies surrounding the King's death betrayed the ambiguity of his legacy to the church in England: the requiem masses which did their best to speed his soul through a Catholic purgatory were the last occasion before Mary's reign on which all city churches used the traditional rite.[1] Soon his son, educated with Henry's consent under the supervision of one of Cambridge university's leading exponents of reformed religious ideas, would provide the nominal authority for a programme planning the destruction of an entire sacred world and the transformation of the religious habits of the whole nation.

What was this world, seemingly so fragile, that six years of Edward VI's reign could cause it irreparable damage? Central to medieval religious practice was a particular view of the role of prayer centred on the mass, or eucharist, and its consecration of the sacrament of Christ's body and blood in bread and wine. The mass in late medieval Catholic Christianity had become the kingpin in a system which provided a

1

majestic and satisfying answer to one of the central anxieties of mainstream Christian faith: how to be saved to enter the joys of heaven. Early on, the brutal Christian simplicities of heaven and hell aroused unease; hell seems an extreme fate for most people's sins, while ordinary life generally provides few virtues sufficiently unsullied to act as automatic qualifications for heaven. By the twelfth century the Western Church was meditating on earlier ideas about an intermediate state of purging preparatory to entry on eternal bliss, and systematising them into the concept of a state or place known as purgatory. Purgatory was one of the great success stories of Christian theological construction, and the mass, as the central act of the Church's constant offering of prayer, quickly became associated with this bumpy but reasonably secure road to salvation. Here was prayer which the living could offer to speed the dead on their way: the more prayer the better, and hence, the more masses the better.

To perform a mass depended on a priest to say or sing it: to consecrate the two elements by prayer, and so to offer the sacrifice of Christ's body and blood. Although the medieval Church formalised a whole series of minor orders beyond the three clerical orders of bishop, priest and deacon, it was the role of the ordained priest in the mass which was crucial to the medieval system of salvation, a role which effectively separated him from the layperson. This separation became such that the laity were reduced to passive spectators of the mass, rarely receiving the consecrated elements, which were normally consumed by the priest alone. The nature of the priest's role decided the priorities in people's expectations of him: it helped if his personal character and behaviour were admirable – to achieve this was one of the aims behind the imposition of universal celibacy in the medieval Western Church – but less admirable priests were no less able to offer the sacrifice. Nor did the priest have to be particularly clever or articulate, able to instil fresh fire in the laity's understanding of Christian faith: as long as he could remember the sequence of actions and words of the local variant on the Latin rite of the mass, it was enough.

The specialists in the art of prayer were monasteries. By the ninth and tenth centuries most monks would be ordained to the priesthood, so that their prayer could be shaped in the specific form of the mass. However from the earliest days of monasticism, the monks' duties of prayer ran alongside the round of prayer and worship maintained by clergy in the everyday world of the laity. Like the rest of Western Europe, Anglo-Saxon England embarked on the task of systematising the church's duty of providing pastoral care for its members; it began mapping out a system of parishes, territorial units intended to be manageable enough for one or more ordained men to maintain an intimate pastoral relationship with the faithful. By the thirteenth century, England and Wales were provided with an all-embracing parish network, albeit in markedly uneven fashion. Clergy therefore carried out their round of prayer either in monastic ('regular') or non-monastic ('secular') life. During the thirteenth century, the work of the monasteries had been supplemented by Orders of friars, emphasising both intimate contact between their communities and laypeople and also the duty of communicating ideas about the Christian faith to the laity, particularly in the form of sermons.

Within this apparatus of production for prayer built up by the medieval Western Church, the balance of lay patronage shifted. The great age of lay investment in communities of monks, nuns and friars had been from the ninth to the thirteenth centuries; after that, with the network of parishes complete, the laity began looking to the secular clergy for their main supply of intercessory prayer. This meant turning to non-monastic communities of priests ('colleges'), or to the host of churches and chapels within their own communities. Benefactions could be made to any church, whatever its status, to offer a specific number of masses: from the speech-convention that masses were always sung (*cantare*: to sing), these foundations were called *cantariae*, or in English, chantries. A chantry could be a separate building, a side-chapel in an existing church, or simply a legal obligation on the priest of a particular place; virtually all of England's 9000

3

parishes must have had some sort of soul-mass provision in the 1530s. Their functions shaded off into a whole host of lay associations, called variously gilds, brotherhoods, fraternities, confraternities; these were designed to further the production of prayer by financing a priest to say masses, particularly for the spiritual benefit of the members of the confraternity and those whom they knew.[2]

To describe the centrality of the mass in late medieval piety is to paint too monochrome a picture of a bewildering variety of devotional expression. The mass was structured around familiar objects which anyone could comprehend, bread and wine; similarly, the medieval Church's universal ceremony of membership, baptism, involved water, oil, salt and saliva. The Church had a genius for building on this capacity of Christianity to invest the everyday with sacred significance. Worship might involve a distant, all-powerful God, but God could be reached little by little through the familiar, the approachable: a picture, the image of God on the Cross above the central screen in almost every church, the image of a saint, the light which burnt in front of so many sacred places and objects. Light played a prominent part: the regular provision of votive candles before sacred objects was a constant concern for parish officials, and the pre-Reformation church interior would be a warm and smoky galaxy of small lights. Worship might be concentrated on the mass, but it was also diffused into a myriad devotions to saints and sacred places, and expressed in a passion for providing beautiful objects and sounds to open up access to the divine – sounds as well as objects, because bells and elaborate music were essential parts of this expression of pious energy,

This sacred world of the English people had not been constructed in isolation: England and Wales were contained by two ecclesiastical provinces, Canterbury and York, each with its own clerical assembly or 'Convocation', within the Western Church Catholic. Between the eleventh and thirteenth centuries successive Bishops of Rome, the only bishops in the West to retain the ancient respectful title of

'Pope', had built on the antiquity and unrivalled prestige of their see (diocese) among all other Western sees, to assume claims of universal overlordship. Although these claims never realised their full potential, they had produced a Western Church which was an international society with its own sophisticated and intimidatingly all-embracing law-code ('canon law'), administered by church courts. The Pope could and did have a say in the appointments of English clergy; English lawsuits might be heard at Rome. The realm of England was not simply bound into the Catholic world through links to Rome; it was also a field for the activities of international religious corporations such as the Cistercian Order of monks, the Dominican or Franciscan Orders of friars or the Knights of the Hospital of St John of Jerusalem. The Catholic world of the pre-Reformation West thus had two pillars to support it: first, a devotional pattern centred on the power of the mass and the power of the clergy who performed it, and second, the unity provided by the Pope. Virtually no one in 1500 could have considered that Catholicism could stand without the combined support of these two pillars.

The sixteenth century continental reformers, however various their aims, all did their best to bring down both. When they read the Bible, they abandoned the preconceptions of the medieval Western Church as to how to understand it; this fresh reading convinced them that the old devotional pattern was a mischievous obstacle to true faith in God, particularly since its emphasis on purgatory could not be sustained on a straightforward reading of the Biblical text. That meant that the mass as understood by the Church was a blasphemous betrayal of the communion whose institution was described in the pages of scripture; and it meant that the centralised Roman authority which persisted in defending the traditional road to salvation must also be a traitor to the faith of Christ. Confident that their message must seem obvious on a reading of the Biblical text, they insisted that the text should be available to all: it was the only road to faith in Christ, which was the only means of salvation. This central message of scripture must be explained constantly to humankind, now poised starkly and without the benefit of purgatory between heaven and hell, and the chief medium for doing it must be the sermon. The devotional world which they sought to construct was thus dramatically simpler than the rich and untidy fabric of medieval Catholicism, and at its centre, in place of the sequence of actions and formal texts which made up the mass, was the apprehension of a set of ideas by the Christian believer, fortified by constant access to the Bible in reading or in sermons. The emphasis had shifted from objects and actions to words.

However, the confused events of the 1530s and 1540s in England produced a remarkable result, which has haunted the Church of England and its Anglican offshoots ever since, and which provides one of the basic complications of the later Reformation in England: the two pillars of the Catholic system did not fall together. Papal overlordship was decisively repudiated, but the old devotional world was treated in a much more ambiguous fashion. That this was so was largely thanks to the idiosyncratic development in the religious outlook of Henry VIII: a doctrinal Catholic who nevertheless left the future of his realm in the hands of Protestants. This book therefore describes the building of a Protestant Church which remained haunted by its Catholic past. A Church which was in theory a tidy piece of theological and institutional engineering proved in the long term to be much less theologically tidy than any other Church of the Reformation.

Much of the conventional historical writing on the formation of the English Church tends to lose interest after 1559 with the construction of an official religious settlement which has survived to this day (with the exception of a brief mid-seventeenth century adventure). This is to mistake the nature of the Church of England and to suppose that to describe its public constitution and liturgy is to understand it. In fact it was only in the half-century after 1559, even somewhat later in some regions of northern England, that the real shape of the established Church became clear; it is this shape which I have tried to describe in this study of the later English Reformation. Perhaps the scheme which I have adopted still looks conventional, marginalising those Protestants and papalist Catholics who failed to shape the Church as they wished; that is for the reader to judge. It is an Anglican vice to make the story of the Church of England the last refuge of the Whig interpretation of history, a triumphant progress towards an inevitable synthesis, or to think of the later English Reformation in a variant of the famous if apocryphal newspaper headline: '1559 Settlement passed by Parliament: Continent cut off'.

Such a result was by no means inevitable: few would have wished it to be so, and many tried to resist it. From 1536–7 to 1570 a series of risings tried to divert the government from its chosen religious policy, whether progressive or regressive. Only one rising, the placing of the Lady Mary on the English throne in 1553, met with unqualified success, and this had the advantage not only of being headed by the legitimist heir to the throne, but also of resolutely avoiding religious issues during the course of the rising itself (see Chapter 2). Otherwise the Tudor regime was remarkably successful at dealing with direct action against its policies throughout the century. If government was sufficiently determined, it could nearly always get its way, as it demonstrated by its handling of the commissions of the peace, the essential instrument of government beyond Westminster. In the choice of justices to serve on the county commissions, governments from the beginning to the end of the century demonstrated that they could carry out drastic remodellings when they chose; often, however, their reluctance to cause unnecessary trouble meant that they did not choose so to do.[3]

If official policy was to be resisted or modified, and in practice it repeatedly was, this would have to be achieved by more subtle means than rebellion, not least by exploiting successive regimes' desire for a quiet life. For this reason, the rest of this study of the English Reformation from 1547 examines it from three different points of view. First, there is the standpoint of the official Reformation – what the Crown, its ministers, church leaders and local agents wanted: this will be treated as a chronological narrative. Second, there is the reality of a reformed Church which emerged from these policies. By Queen Elizabeth's death in 1603 official policy and national reception of it had created a religious synthesis which embraced the life of much of England and Wales; but not everyone accepted that synthesis. The third section of the book therefore considers how far the new Church was accepted, and looks at those who remained outside it. First, then, the will of the Prince: if there was an official English Reformation, a construct of successive government policies, who directed those policies, and how far did they achieve their aims?

I

The Will of the Prince

2

PROTESTANT AND CATHOLIC FAILURE 1547–1558

The Edwardian experiment

A decade of indecisive jockeying for position at Henry VIII's Court took a decisive turn in the last months of the King's life with the arrest of the Duke of Norfolk and the beheading of his eldest son; Norfolk had steered the leadership of the conservative faction for more than a decade, and although the King's death saved him from execution, the accession of the boy-King Edward VI left Protestant sympathisers in firm control. In a further piece of skilful politicking, real power was swiftly concentrated in the hands of Edward Seymour, Earl of Hertford and now created Duke of Somerset with the title of Protector of the realm.[1] Somerset's overbearing tactlessness to other leading men and the disastrous breakdown of public order within two years under his regime led to his overthrow, but his successor John Dudley equally adroitly outmanoeuvred powerful conservatives to press forward Protestant policies as Duke of Northumberland between 1549 and 1553.

Somerset's commitment to Protestantism, although by no means his first preoccupation, was sincere and thoroughgoing. With his encouragement the Archbishop of Canterbury, Thomas Cranmer, could begin the work of Reformation which political circumstance and his genuine respect for Henry VIII's wishes had so far prevented. In the first instance, this must be a work of destruction of what remained of the old devotional world. The Chantries Act of 1547 confirmed the destructive intent of legislation of 1545 allowing the Crown to seize chantries and colleges of priests and appropriate their revenues; by the following year they had all gone. The clergy's separation in status from the laity, an inevitable result of the old assumptions about the role of prayer, was undermined by allowing clerics to marry, while one of the chief ways of asserting clerical control over the consciences of the laity, regular confession of sin to a priest, was made optional rather than compulsory. Royal orders were put out for the destruction of all images in churches: a programme of hacking down statues, whitewashing over wall-paintings and attacking tomb inscriptions involving prayers for the dead which represented an officially-sponsored campaign of conscious vandalism without precedent in Christian England. Naturally, much old ceremonial was abolished, and with these visual assaults came an assault on conservative ears: the replacement of Latin services by a single set of English rites contained in the Prayer Book of 1549. Any defence of the old system or attack on Protestantism was hampered by Parliament's abolition of all parliamentary legislation against heretical opinions.

Much of this destructive programme implied a positive system to replace it: a married clergy leading the people in a vernacular liturgy which concentrated their minds on a single road to salvation through the saving work of Christ on the Cross. The new 1549 Communion Service (with the grudging subtitle 'commonly called the mass') pointedly left out the ceremony of lifting up or elevating the consecrated elements which emphasised their character as a sacrificial offering to the Father and which gave a chance for the laity to dwell on them in adoration; instead, the character of the communion as thanksgiving was a repeated emphasis of the service's language, and the highpoint of the service, instead of consecration or elevation, became the laity's reception of the consecrated elements, now restored to them at every communion service.[2] If the people did not get the point of all this, and if the clergy did not have the heart or the capacity to explain it in sermons, Cranmer had led a team to produce 12 set sermons or homilies. These explained the central themes of the Protestant view of salvation and other guidelines for Christian life and thought, and were authorised for use by Somerset's government.

Cranmer was a cautious man by nature, and his progress away from traditional Catholicism, fortunately well-documented for us by his surviving papers, had been a slow process during the last two decades of Henry VIII's reign. Initially pulled towards the Lutheran Reformation by his German contacts in the 1530s, he was persuaded probably in 1546 to go beyond German Lutherans in their robust and comparatively conservative affirmation of the presence of Christ in the consecrated elements of the eucharist, to envisage a 'true presence' rather than a 'real presence' of Christ: true to the individual believer.[3] This drew him away from the Lutherans towards the group of Swiss reformers who had been inspired by Huldrych Zwingli of Zurich, although it did not mean that he became completely identified with them: Zwingli had been much more inclined to see the service of eucharist from the subjective viewpoint of the Christian believer, as representing a pledge of the believer's faith, and he was reluctant to use any language of presence in connection with the eucharist.

Such questions had bitterly split Protestant churchmen on the continent, and splits were the last thing Cranmer wanted at this delicate stage in his plans; happily unconscious of the depth of the disagreements, he had a vision of building a new religious commonwealth in England and Wales which would provide a bastion to defend a new Western Christendom freed of Romish error. The first test of his intentions would take the very practical form of offering emergency hospitality: England's new sympathetic interest in the continental Protestants would come none too soon. In 1548 Protestantism in central Europe was thrown into disarray by the rigid execution by the Holy Roman Emperor Charles V of the Interim of Augsburg, an attempt by the Catholic Emperor at compromise between his warring Catholic and Protestant subjects giving extremely limited concessions to the Protestants. Refugees from the enforcement of the Interim flooded into England, and provided Cranmer both with welcome advice and unwelcome criticism of his programme.

The scale of Cranmer's thinking was therefore both national and international, and this would present him and his supporters in Somerset's and Northumberland's governments with multiple problems. First, at a national level, he had the twin problem of completing the work of uncompromised Reformation, while not provoking desperate violence from the large section of the nation at all social levels who had no sympathy with his aims. The difficulty here was revealed by a large scale rebellion against the introduction of the first Prayer Book, which flared up in 1549 in Devon and Cornwall and whose messy and prolonged suppression contributed to Somerset's downfall. A similar twin problem arose on the international level. Here, Cranmer had to pursue his efforts at building international Protestant consensus in the face of the inconvenient fact that the Holy Roman Emperor Charles v, both an English ally by tradition, and a present ally in England's expensive war of attrition against France, was highly suspicious of Somerset's religious policy and particularly anxious for the welfare of the steadfastly Catholic Princess Mary, his cousin and Edward vi's half-sister. Often Cranmer's appreciation of the need for caution at both these levels baffled and infuriated those English Protestants who had returned from continental exile on Edward vi's accession, and those continental reformers who had dealings with the Archbishop.

These worries at home and abroad meant that the sweeping changes of 1547–9 both did not go far enough for many reformers, and were also enforced with a certain moderation towards conservatives. To the horror of advanced Protestants, Cranmer so constructed the 1549 Prayer Book that the old vestments and much of the old ceremonial could be used with it, despite the radical shift in its underlying theology. Although Somerset's government harassed the two most prominent conservative bishops, Stephen Gardiner and Edmund Bonner, until they could be arrested for opposing the changes, and deprived other conservative bishops of their sees, there was no mass persecution of Catholic sympathisers apart from the 1549 western rebels. It was two Protestants who died for heresy, not Catholics, as Northumberland's government, genuinely nervous of Protestant extremism, burned the Unitarian activists Joan Bocher and George van Parris in 1550 and devoted much energy to searching out similar enthusiasts (on Unitarianism and Anabaptism, see Chapter 9).

Cranmer's hopes for an international Protestant conference in England to settle Protestant disputes came to nothing, yet the welcome given by the Edwardian regimes to refugees (despite the annoyance of the Holy Roman Emperor) meant that England became a major centre for the developing European Reformation: with the Lutherans ceasing to take initiatives in continental Protestantism and Calvin's Geneva not yet in the dominant position which it would later assume, England had a good chance of taking the leading role internationally. It all depended on how far the government was prepared to let the theologians take their reforms; the crucial struggle came in 1550–1, when it seemed as if John Hooper, an English friend of the Zurich reformers who found Cranmer such a disappointment, might lead the English Reformation to be as thoroughgoing as anything in Switzerland.

1550 was a propitious moment for further reform in England. Northumberland had consolidated his position after the defeat both of Somerset and of religiously conservative politicians, and in March he negotiated a treaty ending the war with the French which left him less dependent diplomatically on the Emperor. Northumberland remains one of the most shadowy of Tudor statesmen, and although there can be little doubt of his Protestant sympathies, his motives in the moves of 1550–1 are dubious. Dr Opie saw him as suspicious of Cranmer's international projects, and ready to back his protégé Hooper as a tool in his own

distinctly untheologically motivated plans to strip the English
church of further property; the result was a bitter clash with
Cranmer.[4]

The possibility of a fruitful alliance between Northumberland and Hooper which might have led to further reformation as well as further spoliation foundered on Hooper's lack
of interest in compromise, involving him in a symbolic but
highly significant confrontation with Cranmer and Nicholas
Ridley, Bishop of London, over his appointment as Bishop of
Gloucester. Hooper refused to be consecrated in the traditional vestments, regarding them as symbols of the concessions to popery which he and the Swiss theologians so
deplored in Cranmer's liturgical work. Ridley led the fight
against this intransigence, and was so successful in persuad-
ing the Privy Council that Hooper was attacking the commands of authority rather than furthering reformation that
by 1551 Hooper had been intimidated into giving way. Dr
Pettegree has shown how this struggle was linked with the
contemporary moves to create an institutional church community ('Strangers' Church') for the thousands of foreign
Protestants in London, a church led by theologians sym-
pathising with Zurich, and intended by its supporters to
provide models for further reformation in the Church of
England; Ridley continued to wage a vendetta with its
leadership, a potential thorn in the side of his work in his
diocese, for a further two years after Hooper's capitulation.
Northumberland's abandonment of Hooper in these complex disputes represented the highwater mark of Protestant
advance, and the 'Strangers' were destined to have virtually
no influence on the official Reformation which continued
under construction in 1552–3.[5]

This Reformation owed its shape once more to Cranmer,
working in consultation with more moderate continental
reformers like Martin Bucer and Peter Martyr, and now
under less pressure to conciliate Catholic opinion at home
and abroad, with leading conservative bishops in gaol and
the Emperor less of a diplomatic threat. Now the theological
message which underlay the services of the 1549 Prayer

Book could be spelled out more clearly, and although ordinary people may have found the changes under Somerset more obvious and traumatic, the much more far-reaching theological consolidation of the new order was achieved now. Altars were ordered to be demolished in 1550 and replaced by wooden tables, as an act of discontinuity with the hated sacrifice of the mass. In the same year Cranmer published a new Ordinal (rite for the ordination of priests and deacons and for the consecration of bishops), owing much to Bucer's work, carefully omitting any notion of a priest offering sacrifice, and instead emphasising his role as a pastor and teacher. Revised in some details in a Protestant direction, this formed part of an entire new Book of Common Prayer in 1552.

The 1552 Book was the ultimate expression of Cranmer's theological outlook. In it, his 'true presence' view of the eucharist can be seen in the way that the communion service has no specific moment of consecration of the elements by the priest, as had remained in 1549; the priest is even enjoined in the service to take unconsumed bread and wine home with him for his own use.[6] Besides liturgy, Cranmer went on to produce definitions of reformed doctrine and law. In 1553 the doctrines of the Church of England were summarised in Forty-Two Articles; but now time was running short. The Articles may never have been brought before the Provincial Convocations, while a legal committee's draft work known as the *Reformatio Legum*, which would have ended the Church's dependence on medieval canon law and given it a reformed basis of discipline, remained a draft only.

As the Hooper affair had demonstrated, the theologians were never working in a political vacuum, and their efforts at reform were compromised by the selfishness and greed of their allies in the regimes of both Somerset and Northumberland. The destruction of the old devotional world meant further pickings for the secular aristocracy and money for the government: bishops and cathedral chapters were forced into surrendering ancient estates on very unequal terms, and the sale of the chantries realised perhaps as much as a quarter of the great Crown windfall from the monastic dissolutions. Many of the chantry foundations had been associated with wider charitable purposes and with providing education. Despite a rash of refoundations of schools bearing the name of Edward VI, the short-term loss was considerable: Professor Cressy's work on literacy levels in the Tudor age reveals how literacy among those educated in the 1540s and 1550s fell back from levels achieved in earlier decades, and it is difficult not to make the connection with this disruption.[7] In the last months of Northumberland's regime plans were going ahead to list and confiscate most bells and a wide range of church plate from the parish churches. Still bitterly attacking his radical Swiss-inclined theological opponents in the years of their mutual ruin under Mary, Nicholas Ridley alleged that they had colluded with the aristocracy in this work of destruction, while Cranmer had vainly protested against further pillaging of the Church.[8]

Yet there was an ambiguity about this work of spoliation: was it sheer secular greed or a necessary humbling of a proud Church? Did 21 English and Welsh bishops really need to have around 177 houses in which to live, as they had done in 1535? There is good evidence that Northumberland's regime realised that the spoliation of the bishops' estates had gone too far, for some compensatory estates were granted during 1550. The government suppressed the bishopric of Westminster and had plans to suppress the bishopric of Durham; but Westminster was little loss to the church's administration, and the suppression of Durham promised to lead to two new bishoprics in the north which might have served the reformed church better than the state within a state of the medieval prince-bishops at Durham. Nevertheless, what cannot be doubted is the atmosphere of suspicion and separation between Cranmer and his colleagues and the leading men of government who were formulating these schemes.[9]

What is remarkable about Edward's reign is that so far the local elites which were crucial to enforcing the government's will across the nation had not openly polarised in the way which would lead to the exclusion of many politically and religiously unreliable local magnates under Mary and Elizabeth. The composition of commissions of the peace and the names of those whom the government recommended as suitable candidates to be elected to Parliament reveal a wide cross-section of those who can be later defined clearly as Catholic sympathisers alongside positive supporters of reform; not only that, but the 1553 commissions to survey church goods, which one might consider to have been an acid test of a gentleman's willingness to collaborate with Northumberland's plans, included a significant number of subsequent religious conservatives. Perhaps sufficient confusion reigned among the gentry to make it difficult for them to take the drastic step of openly opposing the government's will; perhaps conservatives at this stage felt that they could best obstruct the work of Reformation by working from within the political establishment. The government's caution and moderation in carrying out the programme of reform probably contributed to this; conservative higher clergy generally seem to have seen the need for resistance before the conservative lay magnates, but they remained isolated in their resistance.[10]

The struggle for Catholicism

Previously a healthy boy, Edward vi contracted tuberculosis in the winter of 1553, and with his heir under the terms of his father's will notoriously a Catholic, disaster loomed for the Protestant cause. Desperate measures were called for; between them the young King and Northumberland determined to alter the succession to secure Protestantism. That they did not succeed is one of the greatest surprises of sixteenth century English politics. From London to York to Anglesey to Cornwall to Ipswich, Jane Grey was proclaimed Queen of England; but in a remarkable *coup d'état*, Mary was able to supplant her with the aid of gentry in East Anglia and the Thames Valley. In this *coup*, Mary was relying on a small and tightly-knit group of long-standing Catholic gentry supporters, but the secret of her success was a much wider appeal to legitimism and a careful avoidance of religious issues during the course of the rising itself.[11]

Mary's *coup* discredited the leading Protestant churchmen like Cranmer who had backed the government of Queen Jane, leaving them with the taint of treachery in the popular mind and giving the government good excuses to arrest them for treason even before the restoration of the old heresy laws. However, her very success may have given the Queen a mistaken impression of her potential backing. If it had been her legitimate claim to the throne rather than her religion that had spread her support beyond Catholic sympathisers, she was to find that even among Catholics, her fervent wish to return England to papal obedience came as an unwelcome surprise. Moreover, Mary gained a mistaken impression of Protestant lack of steadfastness from Northumberland's abject submission to Catholicism before his execution; not every Protestant would prove so apparently unprincipled. From all this Mary drew the conclusion that all she need do was to restore things as they had been in her girlhood. Even this was a formidable enough task: no less than rebuilding the Church on the twin pillars of the old faith – traditional devotional practice and union with Western Christendom under the Pope – and convincing the bulk of the population that the one pillar could not stand without the other. After Henry VIII had apparently proved the contrary, this would not be easy. But there was more to the task than that: in the brief time available to Mary, there was no one among her advisers and officers who could see clearly enough that building the Catholic Church anew would need almost as much imagination and innovation as building a Protestant state.

Vested interests in the former church lands meant that those great factories of traditional prayer, the monasteries and the chantries, were beyond recall in five years; as the imperial ambassador Renard ruefully acknowledged, Catholics held more lands than Protestants as a result of the ecclesiastical spoils of the previous decades. With their local dimension, the chantries might have been expected to hold more widespread appeal than the monasteries, and indeed in some areas of the north, there is some evidence that people had been reluctant to buy them during Edward vi's reign. However, nationwide, their property had gone to a host of small purchasers, often their previous sitting tenants, thus considerably widening the constituency of those with much to lose from any programme of restoration.[12]

Papal obedience, the other pillar of the old system, was not a cause to arouse enthusiasm, as the 1549 western rebels' silence on the theme had demonstrated; even a leading propagandist for the regime, Mary's chaplain Bishop John Christopherson, in his book *An exhortation to all men to take heed and beware of rebellion* (1554) barely mentioned the Pope when he wrote to praise the Catholic faith. Conservative bishops like Gardiner and Bonner who had accepted Henry viii's Supreme Headship of the Church had been made to realise their mistake by the exercise of the same Headship under Edward vi, particularly after the inevitable failure of Gardiner's attempt at a holding operation by arguing that religious change should not occur during the King's minority. Their newfound enthusiasm for the Pope was a handy weapon with which their Protestant opponents could taunt them, particularly in the case of Gardiner, whose long defence of Henry viii's proceedings in *De Vera Obedientia* was difficult for him to explain away. However, it was now clear that they had no Catholic alternative to papal supremacy.

In theory Mary could have submitted her realm to the Pope immediately, but the precedents of parliamentary involvement in the sweeping religious changes of the previous two decades meant that this was not practical politics. Moreover international as well as national politics hindered her: although Pope Julius iii had appointed the Queen's cousin Cardinal Reginald Pole as legate to England as soon as the news of her successful *coup* had reached Rome, Pole was prevented from taking ship for England by the political calculations of the Emperor Charles v. More urgent in the

Emperor's mind than the reconciliation of England to Rome were peace negotiations with France, in which Pole participated with more enthusiasm than finesse, and the securing of a marriage alliance between Mary and Charles's son Philip; the marriage was not finally secured until July 1554. Squabbles between the Roman delegation and the English Privy Council, anxious to secure a final settlement of the church lands question, further delayed matters to November 1554.[13]

Mary, therefore, was forced for 15 months to use the powers of the supreme headship which she detested and considered a fiction in order to take such drastic action in reordering the English Church as depriving the Protestant bishops and married clergy; meanwhile, Rome faced the facts of English politics on the question of the confiscated church lands. It was Mary's third Parliament of November 1554 which supplicated Pole as papal legate for his blessing, and after further wrangles about property, enacted a return to papal jurisdiction. Only now were the old heresy laws restored: the Lords had rejected a similar measure in the previous Parliament, their suspicion of churchmens' intentions apparently outweighing their undoubted religious conservatism. So it was only now that the Marian Church was fully equipped to do what Mary and Pole wanted; indeed, Pole did not proceed from deacon's to priest's orders and consolidate his control over the Church in England by being consecrated Archbishop of Canterbury until March 1556, after Archbishop Cranmer had been deprived and burnt for heresy. After that it was a tragic irony for Pole that the accession in 1555 of a rabidly anti-Spanish Pope, Paul iv, should have been followed by open warfare between Mary's husband Philip of Spain and the papacy, and by the consequent cancellation of the Cardinal's Roman legatine powers in 1557. Pole was always a man vainly working against time; circumstances wasted the potential of a man who had been noted in his long Italian exile as one of the leading exponents of reform within the Roman Church.

However, Pole cannot be entirely exempt from blame: he and his colleagues showed themselves weak in understanding the need to communicate a positive message, having embarked on the negative work of dismantling Protestantism and tidying up after it. In his years of exile, Pole had not experienced what Protestant preaching had done to England; for him, preaching campaigns were associated with brilliant Italian friars like Peter Martyr or Bernardino Ochino, who had betrayed the Church by turning Protestant. In comparison with the presses of the English Protestants in exile on the continent, the official Marian Church proved itself inept and unimaginative in print, and slow to patronise journalist Catholic pamphleteers.[14] In government circles, too, the defeat of the heresy bill by the Lords in 1554 was symptomatic of a serious gap of sympathy and co-operation between the leading churchmen and the conservative nobility on whom they ought to be relying; few Marian bishops seem to have been active in the House of Lords, and Pole never sat on Mary's Privy Council. His insistence on obedience to Rome was not a popular theme among the English nobility, and was moreover an unfortunate reminder to some of his episcopal colleagues of their two previous decades of papal disobedience.[15]

Above all, the burnings of Protestants which have been Mary's legacy to the popular imagination were a major miscalculation. Gardiner had pressed for them, but it was Mary who obstinately backed the continuing campaign when both he and the Queen's Spanish advisers saw that they were proving counter-productive and urged her to stop. Of nearly 300 burnings, geographical distribution was patchy, with no more than three executions in Wales and only one in all the English counties west of Salisbury. Even within dioceses heavily affected, there were concentrations in particular counties or specific areas of dioceses, like Suffolk in Norwich diocese, Essex in London diocese, or east Sussex in Chichester: an indication, which is confirmed by detailed investigation, that initiatives in executions came primarily not from church officials but from lay magistrates, particularly those who subsequently demonstrated their adherence to Catholicism under Elizabeth.[16] The pamphleteering energy of the

Protestants was already orchestrating popular indignation against the burnings before any publication by John Foxe; the damage done to Protestantism by the Jane Grey fiasco was expunged, and the divisions among the Edwardian Protestant leadership paled into insignificance beside the common death of Bishops Ridley and Hooper in the flames. Might these ill-effects have been overcome by the consolidation of a more positive Catholicism? Pole did begin moves which with time might have transformed the Catholic church in England beyond the understanding of his conservative cousin the Queen. The meetings of his legatine synod, a body which could transcend the ancient ecclesiastical division of Canterbury and York, began examining and sorting out the chaos in the Church's remaining financial resources and took the potentially highly significant step of planning the setting-up of seminaries in each cathedral city to train the clergy. Pole's vision of the Church can be seen in orders to bishops to remain in their dioceses and restrain their style of living; it is noticeable that of the 13 new episcopal appointments during Mary's reign, none was of a career royal civil servant, and few had their primary training in canon law rather than theology, as had been so common in the Church before 1533. Indeed, the virtually unanimous refusal of Mary's bishops to co-operate with her successor, unprecedented and highly awkward for Elizabeth, was a measure that morale was returning to Catholicism; another healthy sign was the revival in the number of ordinands after the Henrician and Edwardian slump. Prospective clergy were beginning to find a career in the Church attractive once more.[17]

Similarly the formation of an active Catholic party among the gentry was one of the abiding legacies of the Marian regime to Elizabeth. Undoubtedly this meant polarisation at a local level, which was increased by the bitterness engendered by the burnings: the Marian government was the first in the sixteenth century to remodel local government by dismissing on a nationwide scale those justices of the peace whom it regarded as a threat to its plans. The energy of certain justices in promoting the burnings was a proof of the effectiveness of this policy. No subsequent Protestant government could rely on the undivided co-operation of county elites to the extent that the Edwardian regimes had done. This meant a solid basis of support for the Marian changes which would have expanded in time, given settled conditions. The regime only faced one serious uprising, Wyatt's rebellion of 1554, and despite prolonging it through incompetence and near-panic, did not have major difficulty in defeating it. By and large, convinced Protestants among the gentry either fled abroad (a minority) or preserved their faith in a passive fashion, semi-conforming rather like their mirror image, 'church papists', in subsequent Protestant reigns. They certainly did not cause major trouble in Parliament. Dr Loach's work shows that despite tensions between leading churchmen and the aristocracy, Mary's Parliaments caused her few problems over her religious changes unless the personal interests of the landed classes were affected.[18]

What these beginnings needed above all was time: time not simply to restore structures administrative and architectural, but patterns of mind. It would take education to restore meaning to the complex of traditional beliefs. Prominent Protestant academics left the universities, mostly for exile, after Mary's accession; the government replaced foreign Protestants as professors at Oxford with its own transplanted Spanish scholars. The foundation of Trinity and St John's Colleges, Oxford, the transformation of Gonville Hall, Cambridge by John Caius, and a sprinkling of new grammar schools with statutes proclaiming their promotion of the Catholic faith showed the way for what might be done by private individuals. The Society of Jesus in the first flush of its success and energy would have galvanised these partial beginnings; indeed, Pole and the Jesuit founder Ignatius Loyola had been on friendly terms. However, once more, time, other preoccupations and ill-luck postponed the arrival of a Jesuit representative until a month before Pole's death.[19] Death was the greatest enemy of the struggle for Catholic restoration. Gardiner, Mary's most able and experienced minister, died in 1555. Historians are only now coming to realise the importance of the great influenza epidemic of 1557–9 in weakening the Marian leadership, in which the generation who had grown to maturity in the years before the schism of the 1530s was disproportionately represented: ageing bishops and justices of the peace were easy prey for the disease.[20] In the midst of this was the ultimate disaster of Mary's cancer, the cruel truth about her last hopes of a pregnancy to provide a Catholic heir; she and Cardinal Pole died within hours of each other.

3

1559–1577: THE CUCKOO IN THE NEST

Constructing a Settlement

When Elizabeth succeeded Mary on 17 November 1558, another change in religion was inevitable; every well-informed observer, including the late Queen's husband, King Philip of Spain, realised that. Elizabeth's symbolic role as Anne Boleyn's daughter, her known Protestant sympathies and her often dangerous position as a semi-prisoner during Mary's reign made her a focus for Protestant hopes, while the growing unpopularity of the disastrous war with France, a product of the Spanish alliance whose main result had been the loss of England's last continental outpost at Calais, gave the new regime an obvious incentive to repudiate all the policies of the Marian government.[1] Even before Mary's death, Elizabeth had shown her future intentions by choosing William Cecil as her Principal Secretary; Cecil's friends dominated the Privy Council which she formed, and with his brother-in-law Nicholas Bacon, whom the Queen appointed as Lord Keeper of the Great Seal, Cecil was to be the architect of a Protestant transformation in the English Church.

The nature of this transformation has become much clearer in the last two decades; it was an operation planned with great skill for the Queen by Cecil and his associates, taking into account the delicate diplomatic and political situation which they faced. Determined as they were to re-establish Protestantism, they faced the fact that England's chief ally in the turbulence of European politics was the Catholic King of Spain, and that within the nation, probably the bulk of the population and certainly the majority of those who mattered, the 'political nation', were conservative in their religious sympathies. A far higher proportion of the French nobility, perhaps half, were convinced Calvinist Protestants in 1559, and yet in the end France would remain Catholic after decades of devastating civil war; so there were high risks involved in what the new Queen and her ministers were planning.[2]

Given these considerations, it is not surprising that Elizabeth's government was very careful in how it presented what it was doing, and that it is not always easy to divine the intentions behind the 1559 Settlement; during the nineteenth century, the waters were muddied by debates within the Church of England between the Evangelical and Catholic parties, with the Catholics anxious to clutch at any straw of evidence suggesting Catholic intentions behind the Settlement. For historians in the two decades from the 1950s, interpretation of these crucial events in the development of the English Church was further confused by a model of what happened constructed on very flimsy evidence by Sir John Neale. Neale's thesis was that Elizabeth did not intend to do more than erect a Church like the semi-Catholic compromise evolved by her father, but that she was pushed into a much more Protestant programme, bringing back the 1552 Prayer Book, by activists in the House of Commons led by gentlemen who had returned from continental exile.[3] This theory was based on a number of misunderstandings and misinterpretations.

First, Elizabeth's care to conceal her personal religious preferences, way beyond the demands of diplomacy, makes them exceedingly difficult to fathom. She would betray her feelings in some matters and on certain occasions: thus she retained a lifelong detestation of married clergy and a liking for beautiful church music, much of it composed for her

Chapel Royal by Catholics who stubbornly refused to conform to her religious Settlement. Moreover the communion table in the Chapel Royal remained vested like an altar with silver cross and candlesticks, to the grave scandal of nearly all her senior clergy and of other Protestant enthusiasts; at least four times these ornaments suffered physical vandalism, but they were always replaced. Yet on other occasions she could be disconcertingly inconsistent, exploding in fury at the unfortunate Dean of St Paul's when in 1561 he presented her with a copy of the new Prayer Book lavishly illustrated like a missal; and her famed obstinacy in the matter of the cross and candlesticks may well have had little more theological motive behind it than irritation at being put under pressure by clergymen and insolent subjects. There is no concrete evidence at all that she wanted even to restore the more Catholic forms of the 1549 Prayer Book rather than the Book of 1552.

Whatever the Queen's private religious views, the shape of the Settlement as eventually constructed was prophesied with significant accuracy in a document entitled a *Device for Alteration of Religion*, probably prepared for or by her leading ministers as early as Christmas 1558; this hardly suggests later Protestant pressure from the Commons. In fact exiles were not a particularly numerous or important group in the Commons with the exception of one or two key figures like Sir Francis Knollys, himself in the Privy Council, or Cecil's brother-in-law Sir Anthony Cooke: government men, not an opposition ginger group. The important opposition, as anxious Protestants well realised at the time, was as one might expect it: from Mary's bishops and religious conservatives among the nobility, who between them initially enjoyed a working majority in the House of Lords. They combined to wreck the government's first attempt to pass a Settlement in February 1559, and refused even to repeal the Marian laws against heresy; it was only after key bishops had been removed from the political scene by arrest that the Acts of Supremacy and Uniformity were passed by the Lords after Easter 1559, and even then the Uniformity Bill had a rough ride.

This 1559 Settlement brought back the official religious situation as it had been at the death of Edward vi, but made three significant concessions primarily designed to placate conservative opinion: first the alteration of the Queen's title from Supreme Head of the Church to Supreme Governor. In an age of male chauvinism, this did not simply appeal to Catholics, but was a universally popular move to avoid the headship of a woman over the Church. Second, royal Injunctions filling in the details of the Settlement allowed the use of many of the old vestments in services and remained diplomatically silent about destroying other items of liturgical furniture. Third, and probably most significant, the 1552 Communion Service was modified in the new Prayer Book to add the words of administration in the 1549 book to the 1552 words: so when a communicant received the communion bread, he or she would hear the words 'The body of our Lord Jesus Christ, which was given for thee, preserve thy body and soul unto everlasting life (1549). Take and eat this in remembrance that Christ died for thee, and feed on him in thy heart by faith with thanksgiving' (1552). The administration words for the wine had a similar combination of formulae, suggesting on the one hand a real presence to conservatives and on the other the idea of communion as memorial only, in the theological style of Zurich. Placing this ambiguity at the moment when a communicant was likely to be most attentive to what was happening was a masterpiece of theological engineering.

However, these concessions did not succeed in preserving the sort of broad spectrum of opinion among senior clergy which had been such a remarkable feature of Henry viii's Church during the 1540s. Already in preparing the Settlement, the theological consultants for Cecil and his colleagues were clergy who had mostly formed part of the Cambridge Protestant establishment of earlier years (Cecil and his close associates were also Cambridge men), and many of whom had been forced into exile under Mary. Official commissions in which these clergy were prominent toured the provinces of Canterbury and York in 1559 taking up the campaign of destruction of church fittings where Edward vi's regime had left off, and occasionally seeing this iconoclasm get out of hand as old religious scores were settled – these commissions conveyed a very different message about the future of the Church from the tone of the royal Injunctions.[4]

Could Elizabeth balance this group with conservatives? She had hoped that at least eight of the 17 serving Marian bishops would continue to serve in her church, but she suffered a severe disappointment when all but the embarrassingly undistinguished Anthony Kitchin of Llandaff refused to co-operate. She would have to rely exclusively on Protestant clergy, many of the most able of whom had just returned from abroad, although she did manage to find a distinguished former Cambridge academic who had not fled to the continent, Matthew Parker, to become her first Archbishop of Canterbury. Some exiles remained beyond the pale: the Queen was not sympathetic to the predicament of the Scots reformer John Knox, who with disastrous mistiming published in 1558 a comprehensive condemnation of rule by women, only to find that it applied to Elizabeth as much as to her Catholic predecessor. The émigrés who had shared Knox's enthusiasm for the reformed city of Geneva also mostly shared his disgrace and exclusion from English church preferment. Nevertheless, Marian exiles who had fled to other continental refuges would eventually fill 17 out of 25 bishoprics – the real contribution of exiles to the building of the Elizabethan Church.

Elizabeth's relations with her job lot of Protestant senior clergy remained fraught with difficulty, since they soon proved to have minds of their own; already in 1559, some of them were expressing their unhappiness at taking up bishoprics which were being systematically despoiled by a new Act of Parliament to suit Crown finances, and more theological worries were to follow. The development of Edward vi's Church had caused much discussion and debate between the English Protestant churchmen and their continental friends, and as we have seen, had provoked a major public confrontation between Bishops Hooper and Ridley; now the Reformation on the continent had moved on, with the steady rise to European-wide significance of Calvin's reform of Geneva. Surely the English Reformation would move on as well? Surely the Church's bishops were the people to lead this movement? What no one could have predicted, perhaps not even Cecil and Bacon who had so carefully overseen the fashioning of the Settlement, was that the Queen was determined not to move with the continental times. Her Church was not destined to move further in its official formularies beyond the limits achieved under Edward VI; symptomatic of this was the fact that the statement on current doctrinal and dogmatic controversies adopted by the Convocation of Canterbury in 1563 and not further altered after 1571 was a version, only slightly amended, of the Edwardian Forty-Two Articles of 1553: the Thirty-Nine Articles.[5] Elizabeth's Church would make no official attempt to grapple with the development of doctrine on the continent since the mid-century years.

This, then, was the bishops' dilemma – and the unique ambiguity of Elizabeth's Church. Her father had knocked down one of the twin pillars of the Catholic system, papal authority, while leaving the other pillar, the traditional devotional system, largely intact. Both Elizabeth and her brother had done much to dismantle this system, yet something of it remained to haunt the Church of England in the future. The liturgy, already more elaborate and more reminiscent of older liturgical forms than any other Protestant service-book, took no account of developments in Protestant thinking after the early 1550s. Moreover, the structures of the Church remained virtually unaltered from Catholic times: without the link provided by the Crown, the two provinces of Canterbury and York could hardly have even called themselves the Church of England, because they remained simply two provinces with no other common jurisdiction. Within them, the church courts carried on their practice with the same archive systems as before and the same reliance on the precedents of medieval canon law; the clergy perpetuated the Catholic threefold order of bishop, priest and deacon, with a fair claim, for the few who cared about such things in Elizabeth's Church, to spiritual as well as institutional and personal continuity with the pre-Reformation body of clergy. Indeed, Archbishop Matthew Parker, a man with a strong sense of the past, produced a history of the English Church mirrored in the careers of himself and his 69 predecessors as Archbishops of Canterbury (*De Antiquitate Britannicae Ecclesiae*) which would have given little hint to the uninitiated reader that the Reformation had ever happened.

Operating this Catholic structure was a Protestant clerical leadership pledged to producing a Protestant clergy: a theological cuckoo in the nest. How little affection the new clergy felt for relics of the Catholic past was demonstrated in the 1563 Convocation of Canterbury, when proposals to sweep away kneeling at communion, the observance of holy days and the use of organs in church were defeated by a majority of one, and that a proxy vote, in a vote of 117. Matthew Hutton, Dean and subsequently Archbishop of York, demonstrated his opinion of Catholic theories of priestly orders when in a row with his Archbishop, Edwin Sandys, he made an unfavourable contrast between Sandys' popishly conferred orders and his own.[6] Yet the story of Anglicanism, and the story of the discomfiture of Elizabeth's first bishops, is the result of the fact that this tension between Catholic structure and Protestant theology was never resolved.

Protestant successes and failures 1560–1577

Having achieved a Settlement in 1559, even if it did not exactly match her own personal preferences, Elizabeth successfully resisted any major change to it. Sometimes she would have to do this directly, as when she acted to thwart bewildered and frustrated Protestant gentry in the House of Commons who tried to start the clock on church reform once more through parliamentary legislation; more often she would be able to act indirectly, using her bishops as bulwarks against change. For the first generation of bishops, mostly men who had confidently expected in 1559 to lead further transformations to keep popery at bay, this was an unwelcome and dispiriting role. Their task would be made additionally difficult by their lack of direct access to power; no active clerics sat in Elizabeth's Privy Council until 1586, and Cecil showed himself as disinclined to friendly acquaintance with senior clergy as the Queen herself. Worse still, after the rise to major influence of the Queen's favourite Robert Dudley, later Earl of Leicester, from 1560, the clerical hierarchy found themselves faced with a leading courtier who encouraged radical Protestants, often the very people whom the Queen demanded that they discipline.

The bishops were put in a particularly awkward position when in 1565 the Queen's attitude hardened towards Protestant non-conformity. Apart from significant personal gestures towards conservatism like reviving the traditional Maundy ceremonies, the Queen left Archbishop Parker and his colleagues burdened with the uncongenial task of bringing fellow-Protestants to heel – moreover, with so little public or official backing that Parker was eventually obliged in 1566 to send out his instructions for conformity under the uncomfortably novel title of 'Advertisements'. As in the controversy involving Hooper in 1550–1, the main issue centred round the issue of clerical dress, which might seem trivial until one realises the symbolism involved: separate dress for the clergy in both worship and everyday life implied a continuing doctrine of a separately ordained priestly order within the reformed congregation of God's people, a notion which cast uncomfortable spotlights over the other, more profound imperfections of the Elizabethan Reformation.

Even though the bishops' unhappy efforts to avoid conflict reduced the requirements of the Advertisements to the surplice for services and full clerical dress outdoors, many clergy who could be regarded as the most active and energetic within the Church were not prepared to conform to such a scandal. Among former exile colleagues of the bishops affected by this 'Vestiarian controversy', Thomas Sampson was deprived of the deanery of Christ Church Cathedral, Oxford, and in a move against the most visible activists, dozens of fashionable London clergy were suspended from work. The bishops had succeeded in silencing some of the most effective Protestant preachers in the country. One of the bishops' opponents even reissued a tirade against the Marian bishops published from Swiss exile, and now redirected against their Elizabethan Protestant replacements.[7]

Amid furious public disputes in which both sides tried to lobby embarrassed old acquaintances among church leaders in Switzerland, the opposition to the Advertisements gradually crumbled, or the intransigents moved on to minister in places where they could quietly avoid the hated surplice; discreet guerrilla warfare over the surplice would remain a constant feature among the disciplinary concerns of English bishops into the seventeenth century. The affair left a legacy of bitterness; some bishops were shocked at the aggressive obstinacy of their opponents and came to place a new value on discipline, while a few convinced Protestant laypeople began to lose faith in the established Church. That former exile from Mary's popish tyranny, Bishop Grindal of London, found himself in 1567 having to discipline a set of London laypeople who had embarked on their own inner exile from Mary's Church by forming secret churches in the city, and were now doing the same once more, against his own authority (see Chapter 9). Most of the bishops' clerical victims deplored such moves, yet here was the first sign that the Church of England would not succeed in containing all Protestant devotional life within its bounds. And it was also in these years that the initially abusive term 'Puritan' was first heard as a description for those who looked for further Protestant change and a more authentic godly discipline for the nation.[8]

All this wrangling should not obscure the fact that during the 1560s all Protestants realised that their chief enemy was still Rome. The bulk of propaganda organised by Archbishop Parker, and the massive work of explanation of the Anglican position undertaken by Bishop Jewel in his *Apology* (first edition 1562), was directed against papistry, while bitter memories of the Marian burnings were much magnified by the massive success of a brilliant piece of Protestant apologetic, half universal history, half investigative journalism: the *Acts and Monuments* of John Foxe, quickly nicknamed 'Foxe's Book of Martyrs'. Published first in Latin and then from 1563 in successively-enlarged English editions, Foxe's work not only related the struggles and achievements of the English Church to the sufferings of the true Church in every age, but also had no hesitation in naming the names of those who only a few years before had co-operated in burning Protestants, many of whom were still in prominent positions: a potent source of tension in areas with vivid memories of what had happened.[9] Foxe's sources of information were better for some parts of the country than others, but his work was a bestseller after the Bible, and achieved something of the status of a Protestant third Testament when the government encouraged the provision of a public copy in all cathedrals and collegiate churches; it is a measure of his effectiveness that there was little significant Catholic literature in reply.

Nevertheless once the government had neutralised the leading Catholic clergy in 1559 it did not act aggressively against the conservative laity. It was concerned not only to avoid antagonising them and forcing them into open opposition but also to retain the goodwill of the Spanish government. Indeed, when it did make one major aggressive move against a leading Marian layman, the arrest and imprisonment in 1561 of the former courtier Sir Edward Waldegrave for hearing mass, the intention was deliberately to attract international notice, acting as a snub to overtures from Rome for an English representative to attend the Council of Trent.[10] Unmolested for the most part, and with little leadership from Catholic clergy, conservative laity did not cause large-scale trouble: attempts at removing them from the county commissions of the peace and other positions of authority met with only partial success given that the government was not anxious to offend conservative noblemen with particular local spheres of influence.[11]

This situation of uneasy equilibrium began to disintegrate by the end of the 1560s. From 1563, politics in England had been dominated by tension over two royal marriages: the vain attempt to persuade Elizabeth to marry, preferably a foreign prince who would be a diplomatic advantage to England, and later the search for a suitable husband for Mary Queen of Scots, from 1568 in disgrace and imprisoned in England: since this eminently irresponsible lady was both a Catholic and prospective heir to the English throne, her marriage would be an exercise in damage limitation for the English government. Quarrels at Court over Mary's marriage joined with a major diplomatic crisis in 1568 which finally ended the long-hallowed English alliance with the Holy Roman Empire and Spain. It was probably these tensions which persuaded the conservative gentry that enough was enough in conformity to a schismatic Church: about the end of 1568, prominent Catholic sympathisers openly ceased to attend regular worship in their parish churches. In 1569 bitter quarrels at Court forced the flight and arrest of the Duke of Norfolk, irresolute patron of conservative interests, and this was followed by an abortive rising in the north led by the Catholic Earls of Westmorland and Northumberland. Further troubles led to Norfolk's execution in 1572.[12]

The conservatives had exposed their hand, but had failed disastrously. At the centre, William Cecil was never again in serious danger of disgrace or worse, as he had been at intervals in the previous decade; with the eclipse of notable Catholic sympathisers, Elizabeth's Court and Privy Council was a good deal more united and Protestant in complexion than before. From the localities, no avowed Roman Catholics were returned to the House of Commons after 1571, and the 1570s witnessed local conservative elites in towns and counties nationwide struggling often without success to retain local power.[13] The government now had much more incentive and less to inhibit it in proceeding against Catholics;

drastic legislation was pushed through the 1571 Parliament, including a major assault on the remaining conservative-minded clergy in the Church, requiring all those not ordained under the Edwardian Ordinal to subscribe to the Thirty-Nine Articles. Simultaneously efforts were made to remedy the Church's defects: the Convocation of Canterbury indulged in a flurry of activity during 1571 which produced a body of modest but useful reforms in church administration. A round of promotions among the bishops between 1570 and 1572 favoured those most active in promoting the work of reformation, particularly Edmund Grindal, translated in 1570 to become Archbishop of York. It was a hopeful time for Protestants after the frustrations and disagreements of the previous decade; yet frustration and disagreement would once more be the outcome.

Disagreement came over the question of church government; debate had moved on since the question of clerical dress in the 1560s. A younger generation of Protestant clergy were now emerging from the universities, many of them fired by the example of Calvin's Geneva, by now established under his successor Theodore Beza as an inspiration to reformed Protestantism throughout Europe. The essence of the church polity which Calvin and Beza had created was a Presbyterian system which came to recognise no differentiated degrees of authority within the ordained ministry: a contrast to English practice. All over Europe the Genevan system was spawning imitations among reformed Protestant communities, in France, Scotland, the Netherlands, south Germany and as far east as Hungary; it was not surprising that English admirers of Geneva drew the obvious conclusion that England should follow suit.

The first person to make a well-publicised statement of such views in England was Thomas Cartwright, Lady Margaret Professor of Divinity at Cambridge, who in a course of lectures in spring 1570, held up the Church of England for scrutiny against the picture of the New Testament Church painted in the opening chapters of the Acts of the Apostles; in this rhetorical contest, the Church of England was bound to come off worst. Cartwright's advocacy of parity in the ministry caused a sensation in the university, and brought him the loss of his Cambridge Chair and a pointedly warm welcome to Geneva when he left England. However, getting rid of Cartwright was not going to end controversy; he had only said out loud what many of the most active laity and ministers of the church had been thinking. It would be up to the bishops to win back the trust of such people by proving that they could carry out reform without such drastic alteration.

Godly laity had not dismissed this possibility: when public discontent surfaced again, it was clear that even the discontented were still looking for action on church reform which would not challenge the role of bishops. In the 1571 Parliament the MP William Strickland called for further reformation in the Church, but his starting-point was hardly revolutionary; he sought the implementation of Cranmer's draft law-code of 1553, the *Reformatio Legum*. However, the bishops were now committed to a policy of cautious and piecemeal church reform through the workings of the convocations, and they were not going to be enthusiastic about this interference by Parliament in their work of reconstruction; nothing came of the proposal. Strickland's second attempt was a bill to revise the Book of Common Prayer in various liturgical matters which Puritans had come to single out as popish survivals, but he found little backing in the face of strong advice to the House from Privy Councillors. Simultaneously the Queen blocked efforts to revive a number of measures for progress in church reform from the previous Parliament of 1566, measures which had probably been sponsored by the bishops but had been lost through lack of time; no one, clergy or laity, was going to circumvent royal dislike of parliamentary interference in church matters.[14]

Nevertheless Puritans maintained their hopes of parliamentary action. A further unsuccessful attempt to alter the Prayer Book was made in the 1572 Parliament; once more the Commons desisted from pressing it, this time after sharp and direct command from the Queen. Yet this time the Puritan activists were not content to let their defeat go unchallenged. Setting at naught more moderate hopes and the attempts to co-operate with the bishops which had still characterised the previous session, a group of ministers led by John Field and Thomas Wilcox produced a public manifesto or *Admonition* ostensibly addressed to the Parliament. Here was a document which treated the bishops as enemies and the hierarchical structure of the Church as anti-Christian, which poured frank scorn on the ceremonies of the Church and which commended a Presbyterian government as the only scriptural form for the Church. Not surprisingly its authors ended up in gaol, the book became a bestseller, and the Church authorities hastily began diversifying their propaganda efforts away from Roman Catholicism towards this new assault. Puritan leaders of the generation of the exiles, even Thomas Norton (who was translator of Calvin's *Institutes* into English as well as being Archbishop Cranmer's son-in-law), were horrified at the breach of courtesy to well-intentioned churchmen which the *Admonition* represented.[15] In its ostensible aim of rousing Parliament-men the *Admonition* clearly failed. In subsequent Parliaments there would be a change of strategy which attempted to conciliate the Queen by presenting petitions to her rather than introducing bills; yet this gambit had no more success than hectoring tracts or attempts at legislation.

A flurry of disciplining Puritan ministers followed; the main impetus was from the Queen herself, and at a local level it was not pursued with much energy. Presbyterians continued their literary assault, with a major exposition of the proposals, *De Disciplina Ecclesiastica*, being published by Walter Travers and in English translation by Cartwright in 1574. It was difficult, after all, to raise widespread indignation against Protestant pamphleteers, however impudent, when Protestant Europe was still reeling from the shock of the 1572 St Bartholomew massacres carried out by the French Catholics on their Protestant enemies. Repression against Puritans was further discredited in 1574 by a tragi-comic blunder of Archbishop Parker, by now ill and depressed at his lack of support from the Queen's chief ministers, who was deceived into believing the story of a confidence trickster about a murderous Presbyterian plot against members of the government.

Parker's death a year later was followed by the translation of Edmund Grindal from York to Canterbury; once more there was a chance of undermining the plausibility of the Presbyterian case by showing that the bishops could lead the work of reforming the Church. In his work as Bishop of London and Archbishop of York Grindal had shown himself energetic in organisation, a good friend to the immigrant communities of foreign Protestants with their Presbyterian church organisation, and an assiduous opponent of the powerful body of Catholic gentry in the northern Province. His tragedy, and a measure of the problems facing acceler-ated 'reform from above' in the English Church, was that it was his very determination to make progress which cost him his freedom of action.[16]

Grindal's downfall was a result of his refusal to give way to the Queen in the suppression of 'prophesyings': considerably less dramatic than their name might imply, these were gatherings for the clergy to practise their preaching skills and ability to use scripture. With interested laypeople gathered as a self-selected and appreciative audience for the public part of the proceedings, these 'exercises of prophesy-ing' were the perfect means of bringing the benefits of scriptural preaching to a Church whose godliness was con-stantly under question to Protestants because of the shortage of preachers. Regular exercises had become widely estab-lished, and were generally welcomed by the bishops: not so by the Queen. The reasons for her rooted dislike are not clear: perhaps the name suggested lurid connotations of disorder, and in any case the Queen's respect for preaching was not sufficiently great to prevent her on more than one occasion from rudely interrupting sermons which annoyed her – perhaps she was merely suspicious of any religious manifestation which had not formed part of the sacrosanct arrangements of 1559. Probably Sir Christopher Hatton, soon to be so influential in a reaction towards conservatism (see Chapter 4), had a part in rousing her anger. In 1574 she was already goading bishops into interfering with exercises, and only a few months after Grindal became Archbishop of Canterbury, she repeated the order.

Grindal's response was to gather data from his colleagues about the exercises: for the most part, favourable opinions of a useful institution. This confirmed Grindal's own conviction that for the health of the entire Church, the exercises must remain. His defiance of the Queen culminated in a 6000 word defence of the exercises and of the vital role of preaching in the church. One cannot but admire the courage and firmness of purpose which pursued this document to the famous and fatal sentence 'Bear with me, I beseech you, Madam, if I choose rather to offend your earthly Majesty than to offend the heavenly majesty of God': Grindal was not a man to let expediency stand in the way of principle. As Professor Collinson has pointed out, the 'Puritan' Archbishop had brooded on the history of the Church Catholic, and had discovered that he stood in the same tradition as that great fourth century prince of the Church Ambrose, Bishop of Milan, who had likewise dared to lecture a Roman Emperor on his duty.

Ambrose, however, had succeeded in his bid to overawe Theodosius, and indeed more than once; Elizabeth was not to be treated thus. Retribution did not come immediately to Grindal, but when it came it was unequivocal: in spring 1577 he was placed under house arrest in his own palace at Lambeth. The Queen, for once forced to abandon her habitual use of the bishops to do her disciplinary work, summarily forbade all prophesyings by circular royal letter. Grindal, still enjoying the esteem of less forthright episcopal colleagues and of many Protestant courtiers, was saved from the ultimate humiliation of formal deprival, but beyond authorising and transacting minor business, his active career in directing the Church was over. The one lasting fruit of his time at Canterbury was the publication in England of the

English Bible first published at Geneva in 1560; a rival to the translation sponsored by the bishops, it was disliked by the Queen and by Archbishop Parker for its origins and aggressively Calvinist annotations, but it was a firm favourite among the godly well into the seventeenth century.[17]

Afflicted by blindness and in increasingly bad health, Grindal died in 1583, and with him ended any possibility of moving the English Church beyond the mould cast for it by Thomas Cranmer under Edward VI. His successor would have a very different style in bringing discipline to the Church.

4

POLITY AND POLICY
1577–1603

Contention in the 1580s

Grindal's disgrace in 1577 brought to prominence a generation of bishops led by John Whitgift, made Bishop of
Worcester in 1577 and Archbishop of Canterbury in 1583.
Whitgift's climb to prominence is often said to mark the
beginning of a 'conservative reaction' in the Church; one has
to be careful in using such terms as 'conservatism' for the
leaders of the later Elizabethan Church, because it suggests a
connection with Catholicism which would be premature at
the very least. Bishops like Whitgift were far from having
Catholic sympathies: their conservatism extended no further
than their acceptance that the surviving Catholic structural
form of the Church of England was not an obstacle to the
task of making England a Protestant country. Content with
the arrested development of the English Protestant ecclesiastical polity, they valued discipline and conformity above
further continental theological adventuring in their efforts
to bring godliness to the nation; it would be a younger
generation of divines who would go further and rediscover
the Catholic structure of the Church as a positive inspiration
rather than as something passively to be accepted. The term
'conformist' is less confusing than 'conservative' for Whitgift
and likeminded churchmen.

However, this shift in the balance of appointments to the

episcopal bench was as much to do with changes in politics at Court as with changes in the theological mood of churchmen: in particular, it owed a great debt to the personal preferences and manoeuvres for position at court of Whitgift's chief patron Sir Christopher Hatton. Through the 1570s, Hatton's influence at Court steadily rose, thanks to the clubbable temperament which won him the Queen's favour; by 1578 he had become a Privy Councillor, and his career culminated in 1587 with his somewhat incongruous appointment as Lord Chancellor of England. Hatton was not a man to view Protestant zeal with enthusiasm: his conservatism was of a different brand to Whitgift's. His undergraduate years in Marian Oxford had been spent at St Mary Hall, presided over at that time by the great Catholic leader of later years and future Cardinal, William Allen; at the beginning of the 1570s Hatton was probably still a crypto-Catholic. Progress at Court meant inevitably abandoning any open Catholic sympathies, and in later years Hatton showed no inclination to leave the established Church; nevertheless, he kept more Catholic friends than was common for an Elizabethan statesman, and was not above employing the horticultural skills of a Roman Catholic priest in the development of the lavish gardens at his Northamptonshire home.[1]

Moreover, if Hatton was to rise as the Queen's favourite, it would inevitably be at the expense of the more long-established favourite Leicester. The importance of this to the changing atmosphere among the Church's leadership was that Leicester had proved himself a good friend to Puritans since the early 1560s, and now did his best to protect them from the attacks led by Whitgift. However, Leicester did not help himself by his second marriage in 1578: marriage was the biggest mistake a favourite of the Queen could make, and from about 1580 he found his position being steadily eroded. His response was to try to reassert himself by becoming the chief advocate of an aggressive foreign policy in which England would assume the role of Protestant champion on a European scale – in this case, by intervening for the Dutch rebels against the rule of the King of Spain. Just as in

Leicester's earlier attempt in 1562–3 at foisting this role on England – an embarrassingly unproductive intervention in French politics – this brought him into conflict with the studied political caution of William Cecil, now Lord Burghley, whose own genuine enthusiasm for promoting the international Protestant cause was frequently tempered by his knowledge of England's financial and diplomatic problems. Leicester's efforts to re-establish his position only led him into further complications. He persuaded a highly reluctant Elizabeth to let him lead an army to help the Dutch rebels, but scandalised her by accepting the post of their Governor-General; to make matters worse, the expedition was as abortive as the French adventure. In Leicester's absence in 1586, Burghley led a discreet *coup* against his influence by admitting three of his enemies to the Privy Council: Lords Cobham and Buckhurst and, as the first active clerical Elizabethan Privy Councillor, Archbishop Whitgift. The following year Hatton became Lord Chancellor. Leicester was only beginning to charm his way back to the Queen's favour when he died in 1588. The Puritan interest never found an adequate replacement for him at court.[2]

It is only against the background of these complicated manoeuvres at court that one can understand the often contradictory strands of policy towards the government of the Church during the 1580s, and the decisive routing of the Puritans in the Church during the 1590s. Yet it would be too narrow to see these Court struggles as merely self-interested pirouettes; they were played out against a background of increasing international crisis as England and Spain moved hesitantly but inexorably forward towards war. Protestants had good reason to be frightened that they would be overwhelmed by international Catholic pressure. In 1570 their Queen had been declared excommunicate and deposed by the Pope, in a disastrously belated attempt to strengthen the hand of the northern rebels of 1569. In 1574 new Catholic priests began arriving from training in seminaries overseas to begin serving the scattered community which had stayed out of the national Church, and also to attempt conversion of the whole nation, while in 1580 the Jesuits, already building a formidable and sinister reputation among Catholics and Protestants alike, joined this mission. 1579 and 1580 saw Spanish-backed attempts to invade and raise Catholic rebellion in Ireland, no less alarming for being completely unsuccessful, while Mary Queen of Scots, still in English imprisonment, continued to promote herself as the focus of Catholic plots. There was no doubt, after all, that Catholics were prepared to assassinate national leaders: the Dutch leader William the Silent was murdered in 1584, and Henry III would suffer a similar fate in 1589. Nor did England seem safe from more subtle Catholic ploys: widespread and growing public alarm at the series of marriage negotiations between Elizabeth and Catholic French princes between 1570 and 1584 showed the depth of feeling against Catholicism which was beginning to develop in England.

In such an atmosphere, severe measures against Roman Catholicism were inevitable. The 1581 Parliament saw savage legislation against seminary priests working in England and Wales, and drastic penalties for the laity assisting them or absenting themselves from services of the established Church, and this legislation was strengthened in 1585 and 1593. In a decade between 1581 and 1590, 78 priests and 25 laypeople were executed in connection with the campaign to cripple Roman Catholic activists, with the numbers of executions still substantial between 1590 and 1603: 53 priests and 35 laypeople.[3] Given such deep fears, the forward Protestant policy could claim its successes even in the 1580s: the official sponsorship of a fund to support Geneva under Catholic siege in 1582–3, a nationwide Bond of Association in 1584 swearing to pursue to the death anyone who attempted to harm the Queen, and of course Leicester's commission for the Netherlands expedition. Puritans might justly claim that they were the true loyalists in the Elizabethan state, providing the logical corollary to growing national anti-Catholicism by advocating thoroughgoing reformation.

John Whitgift did not see things this way; he was determined to impose a discipline on the Church which would not only combat the survival or growth of Catholicism, but also bring Puritan clergy to heel and discomfit their lay supporters. His succession as Archbishop of Canterbury in 1583 at last gave him the chance decisively to tilt the balance in the Church towards strict conformity: this meant drastic intervention in a whole series of localised ecclesiastical disputes throughout the nation. The previous decade had seen widespread conflict at a local level, made all the worse because from 1577 Archbishop Grindal had been prevented by his disgrace from taking more than a minor role in intervention to judge the rights and wrongs involved.[4]

The forces in these disputes of the 1570s had been three-cornered at least: bishops struggling to assert their authority and promote the work of official reformation: Catholic-sympathising gentlemen struggling to maintain their traditional power, and enthusiastic Protestant gentry who frequently looked on the bishops as contemptibly half-hearted and as enemies of true reformation. Three-cornered fights inevitably lead to contrasting alliances: in Norfolk and Suffolk it was the Puritan gentry who found themselves fighting an alliance between Bishop Edmund Freke of Norwich and traditionalist gentry, while in Sussex, a highly effective campaign by traditionalists brought ruin to Bishop Richard Curteys of Chichester when he tried to bring them under reformed discipline. In Cambridgeshire the Puritan magnate Roger, Lord North, waged a relentless campaign against the authority of Bishop Richard Cox of Ely which brought bitterness and misery to the last years of that old Marian exile.[5]

Whitgift's first important sermon after his capture of the see of Canterbury, preached on the Queen's accession day, was an emphatic call to all the obstreperous, papists and Puritans alike, to obey superior powers, not least among whom were the bishops.[6] At the same time he put his words into effect by launching a campaign designed to weed out ministers of the Church who would not give total conformity: a set of three articles for subscriptions by all ministers of the church. The real sticking-point in these articles was the second, which demanded that ministers assent to the proposition that the 1559 Prayer Book and the Ordinal 'containeth nothing . . . contrary to the word of God'. Here was an attempt to sift out not merely those who wished to see the Church reorganised along Presbyterian lines, but also those who found aspects of the Church's liturgy distastefully reminiscent of popish superstition: a much wider group. Moreover, in its comprehensiveness the attack was designed to go beyond the parish clergy and higher dignitaries to those clergy who managed to escape most episcopal control because they held some casual post such as a lectureship or chaplaincy.

Whitgift's demand for full subscription produced turmoil throughout the dioceses of the province of Canterbury; even after all the pressure which could be brought on the clergy, about 300 or 400 ministers, inevitably numbering many of the most conscientious and the most regular preachers just as in the earlier Vestiarian controversy, were suspended from officiating. The Archbishop's reckless aggression inevitably provoked fury far beyond the relatively small group of convinced Presbyterians: gentlemen who had been at university with the beleaguered ministers, or who had esteemed their ministrations enough to give them employment and preferment, felt as injured as the clergy. Petitions from clergy and laity alike poured onto the agendas of the Privy Council, which was already alarmed by the one-sided nature of Whitgift's assault on religious dissent; the Puritan Clerk to the Council, Robert Beale – a former student of Whitgift's at Cambridge – had two furious stand-up rows with the Archbishop, and a deputation from the gentry of Whitgift's own Kentish diocese came away equally unsatisfied.

The disquiet of Burghley and other Councillors resulted in pressure on Whitgift to moderate his demands; by summer 1584 most of the defiant ministers were offering conditional subscriptions in various forms. Clearly even after so much offence from the Archbishop, few ministers were prepared to forgo their occupations or the chance of doing the Lord's work in the Church for the sake of a stiff conscience. In effect facing the defeat of his first disciplinary strategy, Whitgift now tried a more selective and hence more promising tack: the proffering of a comprehensive set of interrogatories investigating the beliefs and practice of an individual minister in detail, and forcing him to answer in full by swearing an oath under the civil law form *ex officio mero*. It was an effective method of securing permanent deprivation of the most resolute non-subscribers; yet the incompatibility of this legal procedure with the customs of English common law gave it a disreputable air which further infuriated legalistically-minded gentlemen.

All this was more than mere abstract trouble-making. Whitgift knew that he faced a movement which was designed to begin the process of providing alternative possibilities for church government throughout the nation: the activists of a potential Presbyterian church. In John Field, veteran of the *Admonition* controversy of 1572–3, the movement had a leader with just the right assets of energy, efficiency, discretion and a wide acquaintance. What we know about Field's activities in the 1570s and 1580s is fairly scanty, despite the considerable achievements of Whitgift's confidant and agent Richard Bancroft in uncovering them; certainly by 1582 the various groups of likeminded Puritan clergy were capable of meeting in the equivalent of a clandestine national synod under cover of the July graduation ceremonies at Cambridge (the majority of them were Cambridge graduates), and these meetings would continue through the 1580s. At a local level, many Puritan clergy met in groups which represented embryo Presbyteries: the so-called *classes*, from which the Classical Movement has taken its name. These might bear little relation to the popish diocesan structures; for instance, the *classis* on which we have most information, that based at Dedham in the East Anglian Stour valley, straddled the border of the dioceses of Norwich and London in a single meeting gathering likeminded clergy across a dozen miles. Perhaps many members of such groups were not doctrinaire Presbyterians, but joined them for clerical fellowship and support, yet in their different ways, by their confrontational tactics both Whitgift and Field were eliding the difference between those seeking major structural reform and more moderate clergy. With the fierce passions which Whitgift's campaign had aroused, moderation was becoming almost impossible.[7]

When a Parliament was called to meet in November 1584, the Puritans viewed this as a perfect opportunity to demonstrate their strength in calling attention to the defects of the English Church. This was probably the most fiercely contested English general election of the century; it is no accident that this Parliament contained an unusually large number of people who were MPs for the first time. Yet we must not think that the election result represented a Puritan landslide. Whitgift may have angered many gentry and clergy, yet the Puritans had themselves aroused powerful antagonisms, which are not easy to analyse. Perhaps some of the opposition to the Puritans was Catholic-sympathising traditionalism; perhaps some was the beginning of a familiarity with and acceptance of the ways of the 1559 Church Settlement which resented Puritan criticism of the Church. Puritans certainly tried to array their forces in the Commons, but most of them were elected for boroughs with small electorates, often dominated by fellow-Puritan aristocrats: where they faced electorates numbering thousands in the shire elections, they had much less success. In the supposed puritan heartland of East Anglia, they captured only one of the two shire seats in Suffolk, and neither in Essex.[8]

Once Parliament met, the Presbyterians did their best to keep feelings running high, systematically issuing further manifestos on the Presbyterian theme through the press of Robert Waldegrave, a skilled professional deeply committed to the cause, gathering in the localities to fast and pray, and up in the capital organising clerical lobbies while parliamentary business was at its height. They also embarked on a long-term scheme which was to occupy them from summer 1584 right up to the next Parliament of 1586: the production of surveys of the parochial ministry across the country. The

Church of England's official spiritual provision was now concentrated virtually exclusively on the parochial system, so it was an astute strategy to embark on an analysis of its actual workings which would reveal just how serious its shortcomings were as an instrument of godly reformation. Yet it was a plan which was as fraught with danger as with promise for the Puritan cause. In effect the Puritan group were reacting to Whitgift's posture of total confrontation with a similar stance of their own, for they were confronting laity as well as clergy; they were indicting not merely parish ministers, but the hundreds of gentry who had a large share in the patronage which appointed such clergy to parochial livings. The compilation of the survey itself represented the proof of a nationwide network which thought of itself as the godly; and many influential people might find that irritating at the very least.

The results of all this Puritan orchestration were distinctly unimpressive, as the watchful clergy began noting with bitter disappointment as winter 1585 drew on. Once more the main problem was the Queen herself, who twice went so far as bluntly to forbid Parliament any further to concern itself with church affairs. In the face of such obstinacy the Puritans in the Commons and their Puritan patrons in the Lords like Bedford and Leicester were reduced to gesture politics, raising debates and bills on ecclesiastical matters which they knew could get nowhere. As early as December 1584 the most radical proposal on church reform so far to come before an Elizabethan Parliament, Dr Peter Turner's bill to introduce a nationwide Presbyterian system and probably the English liturgy produced by John Knox, was swiftly lost sight of after a blistering speech in the Commons by Sir Christopher Hatton.[9] With such protection, Whitgift knew that he was safe, however much the Puritan contingent in the Commons might bluster; it is likely that the equivocal result of the shire elections had not gone unnoticed.

The Puritans had thus demonstrated their impotence to secure ecclesiastical change amid the realities of Elizabethan politics: what were the Presbyterians to do now? Their best chance of capitalising on twin assets – national alarm at the threatening international situation and the nationwide indignation against Whitgift which extended far beyond their own ranks – had produced little tangible result; all that they could do for the moment was to press on with their unofficial arrangements for voluntary meetings of clergy in a Presbyterian fashion, and to undertake the groundwork for better days. The essential tool for this would be a Book of Discipline to map out a structure for a new church, by now a standard procedure for Calvinist churches ranging in size from single congregations to national institutions. The main credit is probably due to the London preacher Walter Travers, possibly assisted by the doyen of the Presbyterian movement Thomas Cartwright – both of them former Fellows of Trinity College, Cambridge, under Whitgift's Mastership!

Simultaneously this necessary but unglamorous work would stand beside the national excitement of Leicester's bid for rehabilitation in the Netherlands expedition, which was fervently supported by Puritan clergy and which involved many leading Puritan activists among the gentry. Despite the campaign's dismal lack of results, the prestige which it conferred on participants was a useful asset when a further round of parliamentary elections was called for in autumn 1586. Once more Puritan gentry stood for Parliament, this time apparently with greater success, while now the survey of the ministry was well advanced and was supplemented by well-orchestrated petitions from aggrieved Puritan laity addressed to Parliament or the Privy Council: fresh proof of the energy and resourcefulness of Field and his friends. All the evidence suggests better organisation and greater preparedness than in 1584; in any case, a fresh political crisis which was the occasion of Parliament's calling, Anthony Babington's plot to assassinate Elizabeth in the interest of Mary Queen of Scots, gave genuine urgency to the Protestant cause.[10] Parliament met in October 1586, but its main concern was what to do with the Queen of Scots, and it was not until it reassembled after Christmas and execution had put an end to Mary's long if self-inflicted ordeal that the affairs of the Church became an issue. It was Anthony Cope, one of an intake of new MPs probably resulting from a Puritan election drive, who put forward the most sweeping programme of church restructuring ever presented to an Elizabethan Parliament, outbidding Turner's previous bill; not only did it envisage a full Presbyterian system and Geneva service book, but in enacting clauses whose brevity was equalled only by their apparent naivety, forthwith abolished all existing legislation relating to church polity and liturgy. One cannot imagine that the group of Puritan gentry MPs backing Cope envisaged this inept measure as anything more than a shot across the bows of Whitgift and his supporters; it was a sensational way of holding the Commons' attention while they pursued the defects of the established Church in a series of set-piece speeches before Elizabeth could gather her wits and issue the inevitable ban on further proceedings. The further advantage of this procedure was that more moderate MPs could thus be irritated by the Queen's veto into giving a debate on church reform further currency, particularly since one of the Commons' noisy eccentrics, Peter Wentworth, was provoked into adding a further spell of imprisonment to his total as a martyr to the cause of parliamentary free speech; Cope and three of his associates followed him to the Tower the next day. However, despite the new lease of life which this gave to the agitation, moderate Puritans in the House seem to have viewed the group's playing at tactics as futile; Sir Walter Mildmay, the founder of Puritan Emmanuel College, Cambridge, was among those who felt constrained as a Privy Councillor to speak against Cope's attempt. In the end the results for the Puritans were as insubstantial as in the previous session, with Hatton giving the *coup de grâce* to discussion once more.[11]

Professor Collinson has drawn attention to a significant feature of Hatton's extremely effective speech on this occasion: unusually for Hatton, it was largely written by someone else, and by a key figure of the conformist ecclesiastical reaction championed by Sir Christopher, Richard Bancroft. Bancroft's first patron had been Bishop Richard Cox of Ely, and it may have been his experience of Cox's victimisation at the hands of the ambitious Puritan nobleman Lord North which turned Bancroft towards a lifelong campaign of considerable success against Puritan activism; thereafter his progress to the see of Canterbury in 1604 was built on his loyal service both to Hatton and Whitgift. In the next few years after the Puritan parliamentary fiasco of 1586, Bancroft was at the centre of a group of conformist clerics who would take it upon themselves with Hatton's encouragement to mount a counter-attack on the Presbyterians by making claims for the institution of episcopacy way beyond anything that Whitgift's generation had asserted in their defence of the existing church polity.

Whitgift's line on the episcopal structure of the English Church, spelled out during his long literary battle with the Presbyterians in the *Admonition* controversy, was that it was appropriate and convenient for the English situation; he did not try to justify it by detailed reference to the New Testament Church, famously declaring 'I find no one certain and perfect kind of government prescribed or commanded in the scriptures to the church of Christ; which no doubt should have been done, if it had been a matter necessary unto the salvation of the church.'[12] This, of course, was the heart of the Presbyterians' disagreement with him. The essence of their case was that there was indeed one certain and perfect kind of church government to be discerned in the New Testament, and that it was Presbyterian in character; anything else represented disobedience to God's word and was a fatal hindrance to the salvation of the church. Presbyterianism was commanded by divine law: *jure divino*.

The innovation of the group around Bancroft was to take up this *jure divino* claim and reapply it to the institution of episcopacy; this was to go beyond the aggression of Whitgift's drive for subscription and to attack the Presbyterians on their own theological ground.[13] The first sign of this new mood came in a book of 1587 by John Bridges, Dean of Salisbury: *A defence of the government established in the Church of England for ecclesiastical matters*. The statements of the *jure*

divino position here marked a distinct shift from Bridges'
more pragmatic defence of episcopacy in his earlier writings,
and the alteration was not lost on Puritan observers. More
was to come: in the next few years there was a crop of
writings on the *jure divino* theme, notably from Bancroft
himself, Matthew Sutcliffe, Dean of Exeter, Thomas Bilson,
Warden of Winchester, and the Low Countries exile clergyman Hadrian Saravia: it took this foreigner and a convert
from a Presbyterian Church to provide perhaps the most
thoroughgoing and uncompromising exposition of the new
defence of the English Church.

The Puritan débâcle 1588–1603

All this came against a background of increasing difficulty
for the Puritan cause. 1588 brought the Puritans a number
of disasters, not least of which was a riposte to Bridges'
literary challenge which proved something of an own goal:
the series of outrageously humorous attacks on the leading
conformist clergy clandestinely published by the pseudony-
mous 'Martin Marprelate' and probably in the main the work
of a Warwickshire Puritan gentleman, Job Throckmorton.[14]
The Marprelate Tracts were widely enjoyed, but horrified
senior Puritan clergy, who were not used to having their
cause promoted in this way; Thomas Cartwright took pains
to write to Burghley disassociating himself from the scandal.
The government never succeeded in bringing the author to
justice, despite the imprisonment and torture of those associated with the project whom they managed to detect; yet the
Tracts had helped to suggest that Puritans were dangerous
troublemakers. At the same time as the Marprelate scandal
broke, death was proving cruel to the Puritan cause just
when it needed level heads and powerful friends; 1588 saw
the deaths of its two key figures, its protector at Court the
Earl of Leicester and the great organiser of the Presbyterian
initiative John Field. Further deaths of key friends in high
places followed: Sir Walter Mildmay in 1589, Sir Francis

Walsingham and Leicester's brother the Earl of Warwick in 1590, while Burghley's long-standing acquaintance with many Puritan gentlemen was a wasting asset in view of his increasing age and ill-health.

A combination of factors was thus helping to isolate and weaken the Puritan group. There was always a danger of isolation for Puritans, particularly for those who wished to press for a Presbyterian system; they could count on widespread goodwill from those who cared about the advancement of the Protestant faith, as long as they did not seem to be subverting the life of the Protestant nation. The spectacular disintegration of the Spanish invasion fleet in 1588 was a paradoxical piece of ill-luck for Puritanism; a medal commemorating the defeat expressed a common opinion in echoing the words of Exodus 15.10, 'he blew with his wind and they were scattered', and it would be difficult to resist the conclusion that if God felt that strongly about England, there could not be too much wrong with its established Church.

Conditions were therefore propitious for a further conformist assault on Puritanism. In February 1589 Bancroft extended into a new arena the literary theological debate already given a new direction by advanced conformists. He used the most important London forum for major public religious statements, the open-air pulpit outside St Paul's Cathedral known as Paul's Cross, to launch a bitter attack on Presbyterian views which was as significant for what it omitted as what it said: there was no reference to the long-established pragmatic defence of English episcopacy that the form of church government was a thing indifferent to be decided by convenience. The shockwaves of the sermon reached far enough to infuriate King James VI of Scotland with its misinformed attempt to enlist him against Presbyterianism, and Bancroft had to indulge in some hasty sweet-talking to the offended monarch; yet back home, he could be sure of powerful backing. It can have been no coincidence that his sermon was preached only five days after Sir Christopher Hatton had opened the 1589 parliamentary session with a ringing defence of the Church of England as presently constituted. In the unpromising atmosphere now prevailing, the main Puritan initiative traceable in this parliamentary session was considerably more modest than in the previous two Parliaments: an attempt to extend the limits on clergy holding more than one benefice. Before that, the Puritan Humphrey Davenport had tried to obstruct the repressive activities of the bishops, not by proposing innovation, merely seeking exact observance of legal niceties in current ecclesiastical practice; neither effort produced results. Both these initiatives savour of resignation to the impossibility of any more radical reform.[15]

Meanwhile Bancroft was pursuing the Marprelate organisation with his usual passion for sniffing out the concealed, and it soon became apparent to him and his colleagues that what was being concealed was more than the production of scurrilous tracts: a systematic examination of a whole series of ministers during winter 1589–90 brought into the open much of the Presbyterian organisation created over the previous decade. The ringleaders, including Thomas Cartwright, were rounded up and found themselves in 1591 facing first the ecclesiastical High Commission, and then, even more intimidatingly, the Court of Star Chamber. It was an extraordinary piece of bad luck for them that simultaneously in the middle of Cheapside Edmund Copinger and Henry Arthington, two extremist Puritans who hero-worshipped the ministers under examination, proclaimed a disturbed individual called William Hacket as the new Messiah and supplemented it with the announcement of the Queen's deposition; naturally Hacket was swiftly executed. What could be better for the conformists than this demonstration of the depths to which Puritanism could sink? The death of Hatton in November brought some relief to the ministers, but although they were all eventually released, their spirit was broken, and the Classical Movement was at an end.[16]

The conformists sealed their triumph by a flurry of harsh repression against Protestant separatism, which could be represented as the ultimate fruit of espousing Puritan opinions. In 1593 the government executed three separatist leaders, Henry Barrow, John Greenwood and John Penry; this martyrdom of sincere godly Protestants, in no way heretical in their credal views, was a curious contrast to the fierce anti-Catholicism of the 1580s which had inspired penal legislation and furthered the deaths of Catholic clergy and laity. At the same time, the change in direction was symbolised by the government's manipulation of further legislation against Catholics proposed in the 1593 Parliament, in order to create the first legislation to apply similar legal ferocity against Protestant separatists. The measure of Puritan disarray compared with the Parliaments of the 1580s was the lack of effort to ensure the election of godly MPs who might have put up more resistance to this initiative.[17]

After this flurry of repressive activity, what is striking about the rest of the 1590s is the lack of theological controversy. The question which had given the conformists their decisive backing from on high had been the quarrel over church polity; in other respects it was difficult to portray Puritans as a danger to the English way of life, and the issues which conformists tried to take up were simply not significant enough. The differences in outlook between conformist and Puritan did not represent the gulf between Calvinist and Arminian theologies which would prove so explosive in the 1630s; as we shall see in Chapter 5, the majority of the conformists who were the chief actors in the conflicts of the 1580s and early 1590s were still part of the broadly Calvinist consensus which also included their Puritan opponents. Divisions were therefore not great enough to make further conflict worth sustaining; once Whitgift had got his way in destroying Presbyterian activism, the last thing that he wanted to do was to preside over further contention. Indeed, specifically anti-Calvinist works were extremely difficult to publish during the 1590s, thanks to the hostility of Whitgift and virtually the entire church establishment.[18]

Similarly Whitgift's Puritan opponents were not disposed to cause further trouble in public; the political atmosphere was distinctly unfriendly. Puritans were terrified by the government's attempts to associate their activities with the apparently subversive intentions of separatism, particularly if they were conscious of the sharp increase in popular unrest and disturbance which characterised the hungry and anxious years of the 1590s. Their useful contacts at Court had dwindled; the Earl of Essex's attempts to pose as the natural successor to his stepfather Leicester, dispensing patronage to Puritan gentry and clergy and pursuing extravagant gestures in the great war against Catholic Spain, were ultimately rendered futile by the political incompetence which led to his execution after a pathetic attempt at rebellion in 1601. Burghley finally died in 1598, but already most of his power had passed to his son Robert, who lacked even his father's cautious favour towards the Puritan outlook; worse still, it was becoming clear during the 1590s that the Court influence of the Catholic-sympathising Howard family was growing once more after its long eclipse following the Duke of Norfolk's execution in 1572. The Puritan gentry who were so important in many counties both for local government and for the sustaining of Puritan ministers in the church's system were becoming isolated from Court politics, an unhealthy development for English political life. Instead of pursuing the national agitation for change which had gained such meagre results during the 1580s, they devoted their religious energies to unobtrusive protection of Puritan ministers and of Puritan activity at a local level.[19]

This abandonment of an active political programme for Puritanism in the 1590s is also perceptible in the change in character of the literature being produced. The published favourites of the 1590s were no longer the Presbyterian polemic of Field, Travers and Cartwright or the knockabout abuse of Marprelate, but the weighty and intricate moral analysis, complete with diagrams of the path to salvation, of the Cambridge theologian William Perkins; his publications were rapidly outstripping the number of English editions of his hero Calvin when Perkins died in 1602.[20] Significantly, Perkins hardly ever mentioned questions of church government: with his work, Puritanism seemed to have abandoned its vision of transforming the institutional structures of the English Church to give priority to the cultivation of the individual soul and its pilgrimage to the blessings promised to the elect of God. Perhaps most strikingly of all, the sustained polemic against the Calvinist approach represented by Richard Hooker's *Laws of Ecclesiastical Polity* met no wave of furious rebuttal when parts of this work began appearing in print from 1594. In their apparent reluctance to challenge Hooker, Puritan theologians were underrating the long-term threat to their assumptions which he represented. If anyone shaped the mainstream of Anglican thought in future centuries it was Hooker, yet his efforts remain a footnote to the story of sixteenth century Reformation which we have pursued from the last years of Henry VIII.

II

BUILDING A REFORMED CHURCH

5

THEOLOGY: CREATING A NEW ORTHODOXY

The roots of English Protestantism

Christianity is based on God-talk: theology. In the last three chapters we have outlined what is essentially a political story: it is easy for us to feel that theology is icing on the cake, that Christian faith is a marginal element in the calculations of humankind. However, Tudor priorities were not those of modern Western society; theology was high on the list, because rightly understood, it offered the chance to escape from the prison of time and death into everlasting life. The vital problem was rightly to understand it. One of the heartening features of Tudor historical research over the last decade is the way in which researchers have increasingly investigated theological questions; we cannot avoid taking seriously the theological issues which then meant so much to so many.

The events of the English Reformation show that established Protestantism could not agree on what it was supposed to be. This was hardly surprising, since the continental Reformation which had preceded Henry VIII's initiative had already become deeply divided, in particular between the theology of Germany and Scandinavia which looked to Martin Luther, and the theology of south Germany and Switzerland which drew its inspiration from the work of Huldrych Zwingli; the Swiss in turn became divided between the successors of Zwingli at Zurich, Berne and Basle, and the intellectual dynamism of the Frenchman John Calvin, firmly established at Geneva after the 1540s. Amid these divisions, there were distinctive English theological priorities, but the English added little that was original; indeed, the English lack of capacity for abstract theological invention is so marked through national history as to constitute a dangerously plausible argument for persistent national characteristics. The one area in which historians have suggested that the English Reformers were theological pioneers was in the creation of sabbatarianism (the emphasis on keeping the Lord's Day special), but recent research has shown that even this is not really a distinctive feature of English Protestantism; those late Elizabethan churchmen who tried to draw hostile attention to it had their own axes to grind.[1] Consequently the theological story which we will trace is largely, although not entirely, a chronicle of shifting influences from the continent, and English assimilation of them or reaction against them.

Even before the Reformation, England was being affected by the continental humanist movement: the rediscovery of the breadth of classical pagan culture and the re-examination of the early Christian writers against this background. The time spent by Desiderius Erasmus at Oxford and Cambridge at the turn of the sixteenth century was one indication that the insularity of the two English universities so noticeable in the fifteenth century was breaking down, and Erasmus was only one strand in the continental humanism which English academics explored; throughout the century, humanist ideals of what constituted useful learning and good education would shape the way in which the country's clerical and lay leadership was taught. However, in itself humanism was more of a way of approaching knowledge than a coherent movement of thought. Humanist learning certainly led people to question the varied assumptions of medieval thought and to propose schemes of social, political and religious reform, but this did not prevent Englishmen interested in the humanist agenda finding themselves on opposite sides in the struggles of the Reformation. Bishop Gardiner and Cardinal Pole can be seen as humanist scholars just as much as their Protestant opponents like William Cecil or Sir John Cheke, the dominant academic at Cambridge university in the 1540s.[2]

Most of the first generation of English Reformers were enthusiasts for Luther's Reformation, notably William Tyndale, whose pioneering work of Bible translation went hand in hand with translations of sections of Luther's works presented in discreet anonymity. One might think that it would be the Lutheran Reformation, based as it was on the support of a godly prince, which would have made more headway in the Kingdom of England than the Swiss Reformation which derived its impetus from the support of oligarchies in city-states, but in fact Lutheran influence was already on the wane during Henry viii's last years. Henry had personally detested Luther ever since their literary quarrel which had earned the King the title of 'Defender of the Faith', and he took little from the Lutheran example apart from his sponsorship of an official vernacular Bible and the central place of the monarch in governing the Church. Certainly German Lutheran theologians were unwelcome figures in Henrician England, with little chance of spreading their ideas directly.

Moreover, the thought of the English reformers repeatedly displayed certain key themes which clashed with Lutheran theology, most notably in three respects: an interest in moral legalism, a detestation of shrines, images and pilgrimages and a scepticism about the idea of real presence in the eucharistic elements. The concern for moral legalism is already perceptible in Luther's admirer Tyndale, who steadily developed his fascination with Old Testament law to an extent which Luther would have found most unhealthy; later, we shall observe England's role in developing covenant theology as a reflection of the same interest. The earliest martyr of the English Reformation, Thomas Bilney, directed his fatal campaign of preaching in the late 1520s towards the abuses of the cult of the saints and of imagery; by contrast,

Luther was so far from undiscriminating hostility to sacred imagery that he accepted the traditional Catholic division of the Ten Commandments, which conveniently amalgamated the commandment against making graven images with the previous commandment to worship God alone, and then compensated by dividing the commandment about covetousness. The liturgical expression of the eucharist in the English Reformation was created by Cranmer, who had parted company from Lutheran eucharistic ideas during the 1540s; if any one doctrine hindered English theologians from appreciating the Lutheran outlook, it was their differences over the eucharist.

When one looks for the origin of these distinctive English emphases, it is interesting to note both their correspondence with the earlier English rebellion against medieval Catholicism in Lollardy and with the ideas of the Swiss reformers stemming from Zwingli. The Lollards approached Christianity primarily as a system of moral codes, particularly esteeming the moralism of the Epistle of St James which Luther so deplored; they had a detestation of devotion to saints and the outward show of medieval religious practice, and they normally rejected the eucharistic doctrine of Christ's bodily presence. All three of these themes were as prominent in Swiss reformed thought as they were inimical to Luther's ideas. It is tempting to suggest that the pre-existing themes of Lollard dissent struck chords with churchmen of reformed sympathies encountering the ideas of Zwingli and his successors; however, the most vital connection to be made for this thesis, the proof of definite links between Lollardy and the English academics who became spokesmen for the Reformation, is the most difficult to substantiate.

The problem is that Lollardy does not give much impression of intellectual energy by the early sixteenth century; it had become a movement with no base in the universities and no capacity to produce new literature. Nevertheless, it had managed to survive the English Church's efforts at its total destruction, and in at least one case, that of Thomas Bilney the proto-martyr, J. F. Davis has forged convincing links between Lollardy and the earliest English reformers.[3] Here the significant fact is the combination in Bilney of the possibility of a Lollard background with humanist studies at Cambridge university; this may be a clue to the direction which the English Reformation took. It was Erasmus's humanist version of the New Testament which provided Bilney's spiritual breakthrough into his brief career as a reformer, and Erasmus's work had the same impact on the Swiss reformer Huldrych Zwingli. The Swiss reformers were generally much more prepared to acknowledge a debt to humanism and to display humanist pre-suppositions than was Luther; they easily forged friendships with the lively humanist academic community in the English universities.

Contacts between Swiss reformers and England can be ascertained at least from 1537, with the visit of Rodolph Gualter from Zurich to Oxford, and the sharp government reaction against Protestantism in 1539 produced a crop of English exiles who multiplied friendly contacts with the Swiss. Under Edward VI English Protestants could return Swiss hospitality alongside a sudden influx of foreign refugees from the more troubled parts of Europe. Amid this rush of international theological talent ranging from Spaniards and Italians to Poles which temporarily made England one of the international capitals of Protestant thought, German Lutherans, mostly under less pressure at home, were notable by their absence. The exiles who most tuned in with Cranmer's thinking were those who sought to bring unity to the divided world of Protestantism, particularly the Italian Peter Martyr and the German Martin Bucer; their readiness to seek for compromise amid Protestant disputes did not endear them either to the Lutherans or to the Swiss reformers.[4] Cranmer was prepared to use Lutheran precedents in some aspects of his new Prayer Books, for instance in the baptism and marriage services, and also in drawing up the Forty-Two Articles, but this effectively marked the end of Lutheran influence in England; already more central to the sacramental ideas in the 1552 Prayer Book were the doctrines of Zurich or Berne. By the end of the century, the eclipse of Lutheranism's reputation in England was so complete that a preacher at Paul's Cross could speak contemptuously of the 'Lutherans of our times' when referring to disgraced theologians at Cambridge.[5]

By contrast with the Lutheran decline, a variety of Swiss influence would persist in England throughout Elizabeth's reign, particularly since Mary's reign brought further catastrophe to English reformers and scattered most of them to continental exile once more. This came at a significant stage in the development of the Swiss Reformation: the shift in Protestant leadership from Zurich to Geneva and to John Calvin, the creator of that magnificent theological synthesis, the *Institutes (Christianae Religionis Institutio)*. The turning-point for Calvin as he consolidated his position against previously formidable opposition in Geneva was actually in the year of Mary's accession, when his part in securing the execution of the radical Spanish theologian Miguel Servetus gained European-wide approval. Thereafter it would be Calvin and his disciples who undertook the most significant explorations in mainstream Protestant theology into the 1580s and 1590s; first Geneva and then Calvinist theologians at Heidelberg in the Rhineland would dominate the Protestant world outside the Lutheran lands. In Edward's reign England had been on the margins of Calvin's concerns, but after 1558 it could not but be affected by the creativity of the great Genevan reformer.

Calvinism in England: limitations and successes

Can one talk of Calvinism dominating Elizabethan theology? This is a question which has recently raised sharp controversy.[6] In considering the problem, one should first remember the handicaps which Calvinism faced because of its late arrival on the scene of the English Reformation. Calvinism could have nothing more than a marginal effect on the major official texts of liturgy and doctrine which Cranmer had created under Edward vi and which together with the peculiar Catholic survival of church polity were enshrined – permanently, as events turned out – in the 1559 Settlement. Moreover, those English theologians most influenced by Calvin in exile were not those in positions of real power as the Elizabethan Church was created: most of the Marian exiles who spent their time in Geneva found themselves cold-shouldered on their return, thanks to the hostility of Queen Elizabeth (see Chapter 3). The first generation of Elizabethan bishops were drawn in the main from those whose personal contacts or memories of exile were in the older centres of Swiss Protestantism in Zurich, Basle and Berne, or in various cities of Germany; their chief friend and confidant was Zwingli's successor at Zurich, Johann Heinrich Bullinger, who even received the rare honour for a continental divine of a presentation chalice from Queen Elizabeth. The statesmen who were the chief secular architects of Elizabeth's Church Settlement, Sir William Cecil and Sir Nicholas Bacon, can hardly be tied down to any definition of a particular brand of Protestantism, least of all Calvinism, which had simply not existed in their formative years at Cambridge in the 1520s and 1530s.[7]

Throughout the reign the alternative influences from the days of Edwardian theological creativity would continue to be important, most prominently Peter Martyr and Bullinger. When clergy in Elizabeth's Church looked for a reliable and authoritative theological guide, they were likely to turn to Martyr's *Common Places* (English edition 1583) or to the fearsomely comprehensive collection of sermons contained in Bullinger's *Decades* – admittedly perhaps in the latter case not always as willing readers, since in 1586 Archbishop Whitgift ordered all the parochial clergy of his province who were not preachers to study one of Bullinger's sermons every week.[8] In the university of Oxford, personal contacts with Bullinger and Zurich remained particularly strong for at least two decades after Elizabeth's accession, and when Oxford drew up a new syllabus of prescribed texts in 1579, the influence of Zurich was still as prominent as that of Calvin and his disciples.

Nevertheless the evidence for the dominance of English Calvinism is impressive. By 1600 there had been no less than 90 editions of Calvin's writings published in English, and 56 of works by Theodore Beza. Dr Dent's study of Elizabethan Oxford suggests that Calvinist theology came to reign supreme in the university by the 1590s; in Cambridge the triumph of Calvinism was never unchallenged, but it was powerful enough.[9] How, then, does one resolve this question? First we need to have a clear outline of what Calvin's system actually represented, considering four areas of his theology: first, the structure and nature of the Church; second, its relations with the secular magistrate; third, the nature of the sacraments, and fourth, the problem of salvation for humankind.

We have already touched on the Calvinist view of the Church in dealing with the Presbyterian controversies of the 1570s and 1580s (see Chapter 3). Calvin followed Luther in defining a true Church quite simply as having two essential marks: preaching of the Word of God and right administration of the sacraments of baptism and the eucharist. However, he further came to insist that the true Church must reflect the distinct pattern of the Church in its first generations which he claimed to find in an analysis of the New Testament. This would create fourfold and non-hierarchical order in the Church instead of the pre-Reformation threefold hierarchical structure of bishop, priest and deacon: two branches of the ordained ministry, pastors (preaching and administering the sacraments) and doctors (explaining and teaching doctrine), besides lay elders (executing discipline) and deacons (caring for the sick and poor). Since this structure was ordained by God, Calvin placed a very high value on it; his view of the ministry was no less exalted than the value put on priesthood in the medieval Catholic system, and he was prepared to rank the ordination of ministers as a scriptural sacrament alongside baptism and the eucharist.

Given this view of ordained ministry, it is not surprising that Calvin was prepared to make a much more explicit separation between the spheres of Church and State than

Luther. Church authorities ought to co-operate with the secular powers in exercising strict Christian discipline over the whole population, but the pastors and doctors were entitled to explain to the secular magistrates what the Word of God was saying if they thought that this was being overlooked. Although Calvin was very cautious about saying that this should lead to resistance against a ruler who persisted in ungodliness, logically such explanation must include exhortation to the magistrate to correct church structures which did not correspond to the God-given picture in the New Testament. Even within the comparatively intimate setting of Geneva this caused tensions between the existing city council and the new church structures which Calvin brought into being.

Because of the importance of the sacraments for his basic twofold definition of the nature of a true Church, Calvin inevitably gave high significance to both baptism and euchar-ist. In baptism he followed standard views (derived from the fifth century theologian Augustine of Hippo) on its necessity to wash away the stain of original sin even in the newborn infant. In the eucharist, he decisively parted company with the views of the earlier Swiss reformers. The Lord's Supper or eucharist was a uniting of a community with Christ involving more than a memorial of a sacrifice once offered; the body of Christ was present in the service of eucharist as much as it was at the same time the risen body which the Christian creeds proclaim sits at the right hand of the Father. This was a doctrine of 'real presence', although it was not the same as the Lutheran idea that Christ was bodily present·in the eucharistic elements.

Last but certainly not least, Calvin's discussion of salvation (technically, his *soteriology*): this was the centre of his thought, since it defined the relationship between God and humanity. Overarching all Calvin's theological ideas, as with Augustine, Luther and the earlier Swiss reformers before him, was his constant emphasis on the incomparable majesty of God and the total 'fallen-ness' of humankind, on which ideas he erected the most comprehensive picture of salvation which the Reformation had so far produced. In Adam's fall the whole human race had sinned against God and was incapable by its own efforts of regaining a right relationship with him. Christ had died for all to restore this relationship; however, not all were free to enjoy the restoration, since the inscrutable purpose of God had predestined only a part of humanity, the 'elect', to win eternal life through the merits of Christ's suffering on the Cross. For the elect this grace of God was irresistible, and it meant that whatever falling away they might experience in their earthly life, they would eventually enter eternal joy.

It is important to realise how Calvin's successors, particularly Beza, extended the logic of this scheme of salvation. Calvin did not concentrate on the doctrine of predestination; Beza did, and pushed home its implications by asserting that God had ordained a comprehensive *double* predestination of humanity, some for salvation, and some for damnation; God had decreed this before the creation of the world and the fall of humanity in Adam (a doctrine known as *supralapsarianism* or *antelapsarianism*). Beza also emphasised that the elect could be conscious of their election. Calvin had affirmed (against the belief of Luther) that Christ died for all humanity, but said that nevertheless when Christ interceded for human salvation at the right hand of the Father, he did not pray for all; Beza shifted the theological ground to say that Christ died for the elect only.[10]

The four areas of Calvinist theology which we have examined would have uneven appeal within the English church. First, with regard to Calvin's views on the divinely-ordained character of Presbyterian church polity, the narrative of politics in Chapters 3–4 has shown the total lack of practical success of Presbyterian attempts to transform English church structures. Equally, the débâcle of Archbishop Grindal's attempt to defy Elizabeth demonstrated the impracticability of stressing the independence of the Church over against the monarch; this had already been shown by the Queen's action in forcing the bishops to do her will in the Vestiarian controversy of 1565–6 (see Chapter 3). Even though Elizabeth had abandoned the Crown's extreme claim to Supreme Headship of the Church, the fact remained that the 1559 Settlement had been imposed on the Church by Act of Parliament with the assent of the Crown; the Church's ancient legislative bodies, the Convocations of Canterbury and York, had played no part in this major revolution of the Church's life.

What also seems missing in Elizabethan theological discourse is much interest in exploring Calvin's eucharistic views. Calvin had emphasised baptism and the Lord's Supper as seals of God's covenant of grace; yet such discussion of the sacraments is not prominent in the writing of such English admirers of Calvin as William Perkins. Indeed Perkins compared a Christian's taking of the sacrament to the swearing of a military oath of loyalty to a superior, an image which is very reminiscent of the way in which Zwingli talked of the sacraments.[11] The language of earlier Swiss discussion of the sacraments remained dominant, as for instance in the Thirty-Nine Articles, where it is affirmed that 'the body of Christ is given, taken and eaten in the Supper only after an heavenly and spiritual manner'. At no stage in the English reformation did language about the eucharist reminiscent of 'real presence' ideas have much appeal; Richard Cheney, Bishop of Gloucester 1562–79, and probably a rare survivor of tendencies towards Henrician Catholicism among Elizabethan church leaders, was unusual in his objections to the eucharistic language of the Articles.[12]

Out of all the four areas of Calvinist theology, only one became the dominant interest of English Elizabethan theologians regardless of whether posterity has labelled them Puritan, Anglican or conformist: Calvin's picture of salvation, and the developments of his idea on predestination towards the supralapsarianism of Beza and other second-generation Calvinists. Calvin's soteriology could expect a sympathetic reception, since it built on themes which had already been prominent in the thinking of the Zurich reformers. There is plenty of evidence for the wide dispersal of Calvinist soteriological ideas. A key text was the widely published Geneva version of the English Bible (1560) with its marginal notes directing key texts towards Calvinist interpretations, but the marginal notes in its official rival, the Bishops' Bible of 1568, were equally affected by Calvinist ideas on salvation. The one semi-officially sanctioned attempt to move beyond the Edwardian formularies in Elizabeth's reign was the catechism published in 1563 by Alexander Nowell, Dean of St Paul's Cathedral; whereas the Prayer Book catechism of 1549 was largely innocent of Calvinist ideas, one third of Nowell's text was taken without significant alteration from Calvin's catechism.[13] Above all, Calvinist soteriology was represented in the views of successive leaders of the Church well into the reign of James I.

Archbishops Parker and Grindal were men of an earlier age: Parker had not undergone the experience of continental exile, and Grindal's theological sympathies were with the more ecumenical theology of Martin Bucer. However, Archbishop Whitgift was soaked in Calvinist theology, which makes his literary clash with advocates of Presbyterianism somewhat confusing as both sides cheerfully enlist the writings of Calvin and Beza in their support.[14] It was Whitgift who in his intervention in the theological row instigated by anti-Calvinists in Cambridge (see Chapter 6) would produce a classic statement of Calvinist soteriology, the 'Lambeth Articles' of 1595. H.C. Porter and Peter White have challenged the Calvinist character of this document, but although it is possible to see Whitgift's phraseology as an attempt to tone down the enthusiasm of leading Calvinist academics at Cambridge for attacking their opponents, the Calvinist frame of his thought is hard to escape.[15] The Articles failed to win official status because of Queen Elizabeth's very un-Calvinist annoyance at the Archbishop's unilateral attempt to decide doctrine in her Church: a measure of the problems that Calvinism faced in England. However, the Archbishop's efforts for Calvinism in this respect won him sufficient esteem from Puritan leaders for them subsequently to urge that the Articles be given official sanction.

Similarly, one must not be misled into thinking that the generation of writers who championed *jure divino* episcopacy in the late 1580s and 1590s were abandoning Calvinist soteriology when they scorned Calvinist views on church polity. John Bridges, the first exponent of the *jure divino* position, made it clear that he thought that there was a consensus on the theology of grace between him and his opponents. Richard Bancroft, who would succeed Whitgift as Archbishop of Canterbury, could use the language of predestination when confronting the Puritans at the Hampton Court Conference of 1604, and personally licensed the publication of an English translation of an advanced Calvinist work in 1598. Leaders of the Church continued to hold Calvinist views: Bancroft's successor, George Abbot, who survived until 1633, was a thoroughgoing Calvinist in his soteriological views, as was Matthew Hutton, Archbishop of York 1595–1606; the list could go on. Perhaps the most striking evidence comes from Dr Tyacke's analysis of the publication of the sermons preached at Paul's Cross, the pulpit under the direct eye of the government and the Church's leadership: up until 1632 all the sermons which touched on the question of predestination took an orthodox Calvinist line: the situation was 'monopoly by Calvinists'.[16]

Areas of agreement

This consensus may help to explain why the bitterness revealed by the disputes of the 1570s and 1580s did not divide the Church to a fatal extent, and why the Puritans of the 1590s were able to resign themselves to pursuing alternative theological areas to the question of church polity. To have a right view of the road to salvation was clearly one of the essential marks of a sincere Christian, and in this respect at least, few Puritans could disapprove of Whitgift and his colleagues. However, there was more to the consensus between conformist and Puritan than this. One of the most useful ways of creating a sense of common purpose was the fight against Roman Catholicism (and to a lesser extent, radical Protestant sectaries); when contemplating the horrors of Romanism or of the lunatic Left of the Reformation, the most embittered opponents of Whitgift could remind themselves of the very considerable benefits which the reformed English Church enjoyed. One Suffolk Puritan clergyman rejoicing in the name of Oliver Pigg had suffered considerably in the drive for conformity, but nevertheless he could characterise the state of the Church of England in 1585 as 'now in some sort flourishing' when he saw his equally Puritan gentleman patron embarking with Leicester to save the godly Dutch from papist Spanish armies. The Presbyterian writer Walter Travers was even more fervently and paradoxically complimentary to the English Church when writing against popery.[17]

Anti-Roman polemic was the common property of both Puritan and conformist; they could both look back to the authors of the classics in the genre from the 1560s, John Foxe and John Jewel, and on occasion they vied in pressing Foxe and Jewel into service in their mutual controversy, just as much as they did Calvin and Beza. Yet the heritage of anti-papal rhetoric did much more to unite than it did to divde: even the doyen of Presbyterian propaganda Thomas Cartwright was approached in his Low Countries exile by a consortium of Puritan divines for a work of propaganda against the Roman Catholic publication of an English Bible, demonstrating Puritanism's anxiety to play its part in the fight against Rome. In their studies of Cambridge and Oxford, Dr Lake and Dr Dent have reminded us just how much energy was expended by leading Elizabethan academics in writing against Rome. The leading practitioners were men who have often been shunted off by later commentators out of the mainstream of English church life into a siding labelled 'Puritanism': William Whitaker and William Fulke at Cambridge, Laurence Humphrey and John Reynolds at Oxford. Their energy in anti-papal literature was a major reason why they could continue to prosper in the Church despite their reservations about its imperfections.[18]

Part of the common inheritance from Foxe and Jewel was a widespread interest in apocalyptic literature: a seductively satisfying way of viewing the relative positions of Rome and the reformed Church of England in history. Christianity's reservoir of apocalyptic writings, beginning with Jewish works and culminating in the Book of Revelation, interprets history as a revelation of the divine plan of justice, and assumes the literary guise of prophecy. Having originated as the writings of oppressed people facing great crisis, apocalyptic has always had a ready appeal when crisis has reappeared for the Church, and the cataclysm of the Reformation was an obvious moment for it to come into its own; the figure of Antichrist which was a recurrent feature within apocalyptic writing could be identified with Roman error, and thus serve to explain how the pure New Testament Church had gradually been corrupted before the return of full truth with the Protestant Reformation.

In the course of compiling his comprehensive story of martyrs for true Christianity throughout the entire span of the church's history in *Acts and Monuments*, Foxe quickly warmed to the apocalyptic theme which had first been taken up in the English Reformation by the older Protestant historian John Bale. He worked out an elaborate set of numerical correspondences with the prophecies of Daniel and Revelation which divided world history since the death of Christ into a series of periods of growing corruption, with the Reformation as the final age before the Last Judgement. The papal identification of Antichrist was pleasantly clinched by Foxe's demonstration that 666, the number of the Beast, could be interpreted across the centuries which had intervened since the writing of Revelation 13.18 to form the English phrase 'A MAN OF ROME'; Jewel was rather more subtle in coming to the same identification of Rome with Antichrist. Foxe's effectiveness was in his double appeal to historical fact and mystic number-symbolism, while it helped that he enrolled Queen Elizabeth among the confessors for the faith, thanks to her misfortunes under her half-sister Mary. England could take its place in God's purpose for the salvation of the world, although Professor Haller exaggerates when he claims that Foxe's work set out to create a special status of 'elect nation' for the English people.[19]

The identification of the Pope with Antichrist was more than a good way of organising one's thoughts about the history of the Church. Such a monstrous foe made imperfections in the English Church seem comparatively trivial; conformists could point to the Pope's expulsion from the English Church to belittle any Puritan suggestions that Antichrist still lurked in a Church half-reformed. The apocalyptic literature gave a comforting and colourful prognosis for Antichrist's eventual overthrow; this was a good safety-valve both for releasing anxiety about the perilous international situation of Protestant England, and perhaps also, if one was a convinced Calvinist, for doubts about one's own personal status of election. The number symbolism of apocalyptic also appealed to those aware of the growing academic interest in mathematics and in the systematic approach to knowledge of the French philosopher Peter Ramus; the Scots mathematician and systematiser of logarithms John Napier actually drew up analytical tables of the Book of Revelation along Ramist lines.[20] With such obvious attractions, the apocalyptic tradition had a respectable intellectual life stretching well beyond the end of the sixteenth century; the endless possibilities of reinterpreting the apocalyptic texts were beginning to weaken its hold thereafter, but the alarms of the English Civil War gave it a powerful new lease of life among the less sophisticated.

There was much to unite the theological outlook of English Protestants during Elizabeth's reign; however, we must not be carried away by revisionism into overstressing the elements of consensus within the English Church. The term 'Puritan' has meaning, albeit an elusive one; hence the free use of it in the previous chapters. A further exploration of Elizabethan theology seeks to illuminate the differences in approach between Puritans and their conformist opponents, and then considers a very different challenge to the establishment theological synthesis of the Elizabethan Church from within its ranks: a challenge which anticipated the 'Arminian' theological revolution of the 1620s and 1630s presided over by King Charles I and William Laud.

6

THEOLOGY: THE CONSENSUS CHALLENGED

Puritanism in Doctrine

'The adversary very cunningly hath new christened us with an odious name of Puritanism; we defy and detest both the name and the heresy' – an angry protest in 1583 from a group of leading Suffolk gentry whom posterity has had no hesitation in labelling Puritans.[1] Like so many terms of abuse in Christian history – like the nickname Christian itself – Puritanism is a label which has proved its usefulness, although alternative equivalent insults such as 'precise' and 'precisian' have faded from popular memory. The term could remain useful because people could identify Puritans; despite their dislike of this term, Puritans themselves knew their own, although they preferred such identifications as 'the godly'. A spiritual freemasonry united the godly even beyond their personal acquaintance, as the Puritan magnate Roger Lord North showed in 1575 when soliciting the favour of one of the Masters of Requests for a gentlewoman caught up in a lawsuit: 'She is ... I suppose of God's flock because my good Lady Jermyn doth commend her to me'.[2]

Nevertheless, often Puritanism is in the eye of the beholder, and there have been many different accounts of Puritan motivation. In a study still influential after three decades, Christopher Hill argued that primarily economic considerations lurked behind the attack by God's flock on the church

82

of the 1559 Settlement. Without dismissing all Hill's evidence, it is important to realise that genuine issues of principle and approach lay behind the conflicts between Puritanism and the conformists; it was not economic considerations which led Puritans to abhor the square clerical cap, pluralism of benefices, or prelatical episcopacy. The first signs of the gap in comprehension came in the disputes initiated by John Hooper in the time of Northumberland over the wearing of traditional episcopal vestments, already proving the importance of symbolic issues in separating the two sides (see Chapter 2); however, it was not the rather complex political ramifications of Hooper's quarrel with Ridley but a conflict among the Marian exiles which became the *cause célèbre* to which later Puritans looked back as significant, and which one of them wrote up in the middle of the bitter clashes of the 1570s: the 'troubles begun at Frankfurt'.[3]

The congregation of exiles at Frankfurt was initially dominated by enthusiasts for Genevan reform, who felt free to experiment beyond the bounds set by the Edwardian Reformation in setting up a Church purged of Romish survivals in liturgical practice and electing its own ministers and deacons; they chose John Knox to lead them. These moves were not unanimously supported, and were regarded with suspicion by other exiles elsewhere; after a series of hesitant moves and counter-moves and inconclusive lobbying of John Calvin, the situation became explosive with the intervention of Richard Cox, who had assisted Cranmer in the construction of the 1552 Prayer Book and was determined to defend such liturgical usages as the Frankfurt authorities did not find offensive. Cox's clash with Knox produced a celebrated exchange which would prove prophetic for the contrasting stances of later years: to Cox's determination to 'do as they had done in England, and ... have the face of an English Church', Knox retorted 'The Lord grant it to have the face of Christ's Church'. Further squabbles widened the problems at issue; the control of congregational funds became important, which raised the question of where ultimate authority lay in the little church – with the minister (by this time a Cox supporter) or with the congregation as a whole? Both sides indulged in political manoeuvring which did them little credit, and although Cox's party had politicked to better effect in the liturgical dispute, the congregation nevertheless produced a new *Book of Discipline* in the last months before Mary's death brought the contenders deliverance both from exile and strife; this book proclaimed the Frankfurt group's independence of any external authority, and the right of the congregation to elect its ministers. Indecisive and rather uninvitingly petty as these confrontations had been, they opened up the areas which would become so contentious in Elizabeth's Church: liturgy and liturgical dress, and the polity under which the Church should be governed.

It was Cox and his friends who found themselves the new establishment on their return in 1558–9, and their opponents already cast as troublemakers. Yet as their common exile had shown, what both sides wanted to do was to create a Church which would bring salvation to England and uproot popery; this continued to be the preoccupation of Puritan and conformist alike. Both sides appealed to Biblical authority in this task, but Puritans were more singleminded in their pursuit of Biblical guidance. Since large tracts of the Old Testament were devoted to long and detailed descriptions of ceremonial and the construction of sacred objects and buildings for the Jewish cult, it was not unreasonable to suppose that the new revelation of Christ in the New Testament, if read carefully, contained equally precise and detailed regulations for the setting up of the Christian Church. We have already seen that this led to a fundamental disagreement between conformists like Archbishop Whitgift and advocates of a Presbyterian system on Calvinist lines: Whitgift's devotion to Biblical truth did not force him to seek such detailed guidance, and he could not sympathise with those who claimed to have found it. Between conformists and Puritans there lay a great gap of comprehension which the exchange between Cox and Knox at Frankfurt had already revealed.

J.S. Coolidge has pointed to another useful way of understanding this division, by exploring the two sides' different
understandings of the concept of 'edification' in the
Church.[4]

The word 'edification' is an attempt to translate into
Latinate English a rather idiosyncratic Greek usage in the
New Testament epistles centred on the idea of building and
buildings. Drawing on the rich imagery of Temple-building
in the Old Testament, Paul could refer to the Christian
community at Corinth as 'God's building' or 'the temple of
the living God', and the author of 1 Peter talks of the
congregation which he is addressing as 'lively stones . . . a
spiritual house'.[5] The key use of concepts translatable as
'edify' or 'edification' comes in the letter to the Ephesians, in
which the writer (Paul or one of his disciples) develops an
elaborate metaphor of his readers as part of a structure
actually alive, *'built* upon the foundation of the apostles and
prophets, Jesus Christ himself being the chief cornerstone, in
whom all the *building* coupled together groweth into an holy
temple in the Lord; in whom ye are also *built together* to be the
habitation of God by the Spirit' (Ephesians 2.19–22).
Moreover, this building of a community was not merely a
matter of professing the risen Christ and sticking together:
the way in which the Church behaved would itself make or
break the weaker members. 1 Corinthians 8 is a discussion of
Christians eating food dedicated to idols, in which the same
word with the 'building' root is used at verse 10 to describe
how a weak member of the Christian community might be
'boldened' by bad example from within the fellowship to
indulge in eating such tainted food himself. Conversely,
everything about the practice of the community should be
helpful to everyone: in worship 'let all things be done unto
edifying' (1 Corinthians 14.26).

It is necessary to set out these texts because they exactly
rehearse the Puritan attitude to the Church. For the Puritans, the Church was as new as it had been in the generation
of the Apostle Paul, and the same rules applied to the way it
was built up. It was a structure, but one which was alive and

growing because it was composed of the 'lively stones' of the elect; it was not primarily something which could be identified simply with the visible Church, otherwise the Church of Rome (which had been all too visible for at least a thousand years) could claim to be the true Church. The liturgy and the structure of the established English Church had manifest flaws which corresponded to Paul's warnings against eating meat offered to idols, for they had been offered to popish idolatry in times past. In the liturgy, the sign of the cross in baptism, the giving of a ring in marriage and of course the hated surplice were prime scapegoats for such hostility; in church structure, it was difficult for a Puritan to believe that such imperfections as the non-residence of ministers with pastoral charge, or the holding of more than one pastoral charge in plurality, helped to edify or build up the Christian believer.

Above all, the fact that not all the Church's ministers were licensed to preach, or even had the capacity and will to do so, was a fatal stumbling-block to edification. Scripture was the key to salvation, but the Puritan believed that it remained a sealed book until instructed preaching opened it up, ending ignorance while avoiding the misinterpretations of misguided fanatics. It was not enough to read scripture, to hear it read publicly in worship or even to hear a set sermon from the official collection of homilies; a congregation's personal encounter with the living God was to be reached through their preacher's own struggle with God's Word. Preaching was the heart of edification.[6] A Calvinist must also consider those whose election to salvation was hidden or dormant: it was the duty of the church to expose everyone to God's Word so that all the elect could hear it, which meant that every parish must be properly supplied with preaching. Only thus could the full number of the elect be built up.

For a conformist, this interpretation of the word 'edification' as the building of a spiritual community was perversely precise; it was making too much of what was merely a metaphor. Conformist discussion of 'edification' gave the word a wider and vaguer meaning more akin to the way in which we use it now, defining it as that which improves or instructs: so the process of edification was much more diffused, ranging alongside preaching, the public and private reading of scripture and public and private prayer. Moreover, the conformist was disposed to appeal to another powerful theme within the New Testament epistle literature: that of order and obedience to earthly powers which derived their authority from and mirrored the powers of heaven. Stereotyped lists of those owed and owing due obedience recur in various epistles, while the classic text of the theme is Romans 13.1: 'Let every soul be subject unto the higher powers: for there is no power but of God'. In the clash between the principle of submission to Christian governments and the principle of edification, the conformist insisted that submission and order must come first: that edification could only be established by creating a due order. Ceremonies and prayer must be regulated, and preaching approved; this was the responsibility of the state, now that Christian states had been created. It was not for the living stones to rise up and criticise the arrangements on which Elizabeth I had decided: to do that would be to confuse the demands of their own consciences, which were God's gifts for their personal edification to salvation, with the external discipline which God had given into the hands of a godly monarch to rule the whole national church.[7]

The events of the early 1590s culminating in the humiliation of the Presbyterians in Star Chamber, were perhaps an inevitable outcome of this clash of approaches. Professor Coolidge points out that when William Perkins came to discuss edification in the course of his writings on morality, he avoided all the central scriptural texts on the subjects reviewed above, and redirected the idea of edification towards personal morality; the community dimension in it was now devoted to the end of creating peace and harmony. This was a far cry from the strife over edification which had divided Puritans like Cartwright and Robert Crowley from conformists like Archbishops Parker and Whitgift or John Bridges.[8] Yet even the shift represented by Perkins's more pacific Calvinism does not mean the end of all differences between conformists and Puritans. In Chapter 5 we saw that there was broad agreement among the divines of the Elizabethan Church over Calvinist soteriology and its assumption of predestination, but this belief in predestination could have widely differing theological consequences.

R.T. Kendall first drew attention to the part which the writings of Perkins played in developing an 'experimental' Calvinist piety, and from this Kendall pointed a distinction between 'experimental' and 'credal' predestinarianism.[9] Perkins's starting-point was an idea of Calvin's which he took up and made peculiarly his own: that some of those whom God has chosen to reprobate (that is, irrevocably condemn) to damnation are given *temporary* faith which may stay with them for some time, perhaps even for a lifetime, but is completely different from the *saving* faith of the elect. It is an unattractive doctrine, although one can see how pastoral experience might drive a minister to embrace it through exasperation at unctuousness or self-righteousness among his flock. However, it had a necessary corollary in a doctrine of assurance: the claim that individuals were capable of discerning that their own faith was of the saving rather than of the temporary variety. This discernment came from an experience of true belief, or was, in Perkins's phrase, 'experimental'. It is understandable that Perkins concentrated on moral issues and personal piety, given this idea at the heart of his thought, and it is also apparent that it must make questions of election and predestination central to one's religious life; each individual believer is forced to come to a conclusion about his or her experience of belief. Experimental Calvinist piety would encourage separation, either to find groups of the likeminded within the established Church, or to withdraw completely from the community which seemed to contain so many with no consciousness of election.

Leading churchmen like Whitgift, playing their part in a Church committed to pastoral care of an entire nation, would not be inclined to develop their acceptance of predestinarian doctrine in an experimental fashion; it would be an unwelcome complication to their task. Queen Elizabeth had committed care of the visible Church in England to them; their Calvinism told them that not everyone was part of the elect, yet they were not prepared to limit membership of the visible Church to those who were visibly godly. Hence they were not prepared to put predestination at the centre of their thoughts; their predestinarianism would remain 'credal', merely accepting predestination as one aspect of the whole range of Christian doctrine. Whitgift was perfectly prepared to accept that there was an invisible Church of the elect, but he insisted that this was not and could not be the same as the visible Church over which he presided by the Queen's appointment. Indeed, Whitgift could put predestinarian doctrine to what his opponents must have found outrageous uses; on one occasion in his literary debate with Cartwright he defended pluralism by referring to the Calvinist doctrine of perseverance of the elect – once the elect in one place had heard the Word of God, they could not fall from grace again, and so their minister was perfectly justified in seeking fresh flocks to shepherd once he had preached to them.[10]

Logical systems have a way of creating logical byways, and Whitgift's deductions were not the only unexpected fruit of predestinarian views. Experimental Calvinism unwittingly led those who embraced it back towards a doctrine of works, because it constantly focused the attention on the search for visible proofs of election. Calvinists faced the problem which confronts all followers of the proposition that the just shall live by faith; if one rejects the role of human works in the approach to God, what is the point of leading a good life? It was a debate as bitter between Pelagius and Augustine in the fifth century as between Luther or Calvin and their Catholic opponents in the sixteenth. Those who wished to give a positive place to human endeavours could accuse their opponents of antinomianism, the rejection of all rules of good conduct: a potent argument in the sixteenth century, conjuring memories of the licentious parody of ordinary society set up in the German city of Münster by militant Anabaptists in 1533–5.

One consequence for Protestant thinkers was a nervous return to the regulations provided supposedly through Moses for the ancient Israelites in the first five books of the Old Testament, trying to sift out from them what could be described as permanent moral law; among major continental thinkers, only Luther was completely immune from such interests in Mosaic law, and among English divines the tendency was already visible in William Tyndale's Biblical work in the earliest days of the Reformation.[11] In this consideration of Mosaic law, Tyndale was attracted by the related Old Testament motif of covenant, a contract between God and his people, and from mid-century it was this covenant theme which was increasingly used to provide a systematic answer to the Protestant dilemma about works. It evolved into a distinctive covenant or 'federal' theology (*foedus* = covenant).

As with the idea of edification, it is important to be aware of the complex Biblical material involved, which made the covenant theme a particularly fruitful one because of its adaptability; there are many varieties of covenant envisaged in the Old Testament. Some are conditional, like that between God and Adam in the Garden of Eden before the Fall (Genesis 2.15–17), between God and Abraham in Genesis 17, or that covenant announced by Moses to Israel in the books from Exodus to Deuteronomy – in other words, God makes promises in return for obedience. Others are unconditional, like that between God and Noah after the Flood (Genesis 9.8–17), between God and Abraham in Genesis 15.18, or God and King David in 2 Samuel 23.5: God grants blessings without asking a return. Already in the crisis of the first century Christian split from Judaism, the Apostle Paul had seized on the ambiguities of this covenant material and drew on it selectively to point a contrast between the demands of God's law and the gifts of God's grace: humankind after the Fall was incapable of fulfilling the conditional covenant by works, so God opened the road to salvation through an unconditional covenant of grace (key texts here are Romans 1–11 and Galatians 3–5).

Early expressions of the covenant theme in Tyndale and Swiss reformers like Zwingli and Bullinger tended to express its conditional side, for their concern was both to establish renewed patterns of behaviour away from Romish error and to guard against accusations of antinomianism. As Protestantism established its position and began to develop well-settled national churches, interest grew in the unconditional texts, which would indicate God's blessings on the recovery of Gospel purity. This led to a theology which contrasted a conditional covenant of works superseded by an unconditional covenant of grace, a motif which is first found in the work of Calvinist theologians at Heidelberg in the middle years of the century, principally Zacharias Ursinus, Kaspar Olevianus and Girolamo Zanchius.

Books by the Heidelberg theologians were appearing in English by the 1580s (the Heidelberg catechism of Ursinus and Olevianus had been published in English in 1572), and in 1585 there appeared the first statement of fully-fledged covenant theology with a book by the young English theologian Dudley Fenner, *Sacra Theologia*: a great rarity in Elizabethan English divinity as a work of systematic theology. Fenner was the first theologian specifically to mention a covenant of works (*foedus operum*) which could be identified with the Adamic and Mosaic covenants and contrasted in a Pauline manner with Abraham's covenant of grace; the elect were given faith through the covenant of grace, just as Abraham had been given it. Thereafter the idea became characteristic of English Puritan theologians such as Perkins.[12]

Covenant theology raised as many problems as it solved. Although it evolved as a safeguard against antinomianism, the covenant of grace was in constant danger of being pushed in the opposite direction and being turned into a covenant of works, through over-emphasis on works as the product of faith. There was a further danger to avoid. Covenant theologians must beware seeing faith itself as a condition of the covenant and not as a gift from God: the covenant idea should 'settle the soul in peace', as one covenant theologian put it, unlike the papist theology of penance. The realisation of infirmities should not make the elect doubt, but spur them on to works of sanctification; however, once more this meant that in practice, works became of prime importance. There was a further disadvantage in the covenant system; like all predestinarian doctrines it tended to reduce the significance of Christ's work on the Cross to a formality, almost displaced by the role of the covenant itself. In comparison with Calvin, covenant theologians and English Puritans generally wrote little about the value of the incarnation of Jesus Christ, or about the problems of Christ's nature (christology) which had so exercised the early Church.[13]

Why, then, did the covenant idea prove so popular particularly to English Puritan theologians after the 1580s? Clearly it helped to provide assurance of election in a predestinarian system which might easily lead to doubt and despair. It also provided a route to salvation alternative to the Catholic system based on the power of sacraments and the legitimacy of apostolic succession. Emphasising as they did personal experience and individual search for assurance, the English covenant theologians almost inevitably marginalised the role of sacraments (in this departing markedly from Calvin's ideas): sacraments were to be seen as general vows of the elect alongside the particular vows that an individual might make. The notion of edification made the Puritans suspicious of the institutions of the visible Church continuing from generation to generation; rather than progressing by building towards perfection, the visible Church had manifestly declined towards popery. The covenant of grace could be seen as an alternative source of ecclesiastical continuity to apostolic succession: first made with Abraham, the covenant was also made with all his spiritual descendants in every age, who were to be identified with the elect. Because the covenant was with a people, it emphasised the corporate solidarity of the elect, gave them an identity as the visible saints, and pointed to their common membership of the invisible Church: an ideal outlook for voluntary societies who cared little for the structures of the Church by law established. It was not surprising that in the seventeenth century so many enthusiasts for the covenant notion would repudiate the visible Church of England and embrace separatism (see Chapter 9).

An alternative theology

The English predestinarian consensus thus contained distinct conformist and Puritan identities, but it also faced a far more radical challenge within the bounds of the Church: an entirely different approach to the problems of theology. It is important to realise that the aggressive championing of *jure divino* episcopacy by the generation of Bridges, Bancroft, Saravia and Sutcliffe did not represent part of this new approach, although the *jure divino* theme would merge with the new theological preoccupations. Bancroft and his sympathisers were working within the predestinarian consensus, within the limits of the English variety of Calvinism as we have surveyed it, and they were not prepared to un-church continental Churches. After all, Calvin himself had never explicitly said that discipline, that is, Presbyterian church government, formed a third mark of a true Church alongside administration of the sacraments and preaching of the word; while so enthusiastic a proponent of *jure divino* episcopacy as Hadrian Saravia never said that continental Presbyterian Churches did not have true ministries, and himself ministered in the Church of England apparently without being reordained by a bishop.[14]

The more fundamental challenge to mainstream Elizabethan theology assumed several forms, which together represented a new way of looking at the English church: a discovery that despite all the assumptions of the Reformation founders of that Church, it had retained a Catholic character. The Elizabethan Church settlement had created a cuckoo in a nest, a Protestant theological system and a Protestant programme for national salvation sheltering within a largely pre-Reformation Catholic church structure; now the structure was beginning to reassert its fascination, and arousing theological interest in the Catholicism which had created it. As the most elaborate form of liturgy to be found among the Churches of the Protestant Reformation, the Book of Common Prayer also pulled in the same direction. As a result, a number of churchmen began rejecting the assumptions of predestinarian theology and emphasising the role of the sacraments in the Church's life, in particular the importance of the eucharist; they sought a wider view of what constituted theological authority within the Church, especially stressing the role which reason and tradition played alongside scripture. Their re-evaluation of the Church's past led them to concentrate on the theological writings of earlier centuries to the virtual exclusion of the work of the reformers. Taken together, all this constituted an attempt at theological revolution, with two main agents; a group of churchmen whom later political events labelled somewhat misleadingly as 'Arminian', and one individual writer of genius, Richard Hooker.

First the Arminians: they take their label from the continental theologian Jacobus Arminius, who tried to lead a reaction within the Dutch Church against the theology of Beza's developed Calvinism; rather than denying predestination as such, Arminius maintained that God's grace could be resisted by the individual human. The problems with the label are evident if one realises that the English 'Arminians' were already developing their ideas in the 1580s, while their first contacts with Arminius seem to date from the 1590s; furthermore, the interests of the English 'Arminians' developed away from the predestination debate towards the value of the sacraments and the nature of the Church.[15] If we use the label 'Arminian' for English Churchmen, it must be with these important qualifications in mind; 'proto-Arminian' would be a more accurate term.

The first stirrings of proto-Arminianism were in the two

universities, where it was somewhat safer to express dissenting views than elsewhere: Samuel Harsnet's attempt to use the London pulpit of Paul's Cross for criticism of Calvinism in 1584 was sternly rebuked by Archbishop Whitgift. Nevertheless, even in the universities theological diversity faced grave dangers. From 1576 Oxford witnessed a mounting attack on Antonio del Corro, a free-thinking former Spanish monk and bizarrely enough a protégé of the Earl of Leicester, who dared to criticise the doctrine of predestination; Corro was finally silenced in 1586, and seems to have found no disciples in Oxford, which exhibited no further tendencies to Arminian ideas until after the turn of the century.[16] Cambridge began rather later, but maintained a continuous proto-Arminian presence in the face of attempts at suppression. The first significant figure was the future bishop Lancelot Andrewes, a fellow of Pembroke College from 1575; as Master of Pembroke from 1589 and an increasingly popular Court preacher, Andrewes was in a strong position to protect himself and to encourage others, although his peacable nature prevented him from much active confrontation with the Calvinists. During the 1580s Andrewes emerged as a distinctive figure; the whole style of his preaching and theological writing marked him off from the mainstream, largely ignoring the work of the sixteenth century reformers to concentrate on the writings of Fathers of the early Church, and stressing the role of human reason in appropriating the truths of Christianity.

Andrewes did his best to defend proto-Arminians when a full-scale row broke out in Cambridge in 1595. William Barrett, chaplain of Gonville and Caius College, had the audacity to preach a university sermon which not only attacked predestinarianism but Calvin himself; he was probably influenced by the anti-Calvinist views of the Lady Margaret Professor, the Frenchman Peter Baro, yet another continental exile to disturb the Elizabethan theological consensus. Disciplined by the university authorities, Barrett appealed to Archbishop Whitgift, whose response was the thoroughgoing Calvinism of the Lambeth Articles (see Chapter 5); despite the intervention of Andrewes and other sympathisers, Barrett's Cambridge career was ruined, and he ended his days as a Roman Catholic layman. However, other Cambridge anti-Calvinists persisted; Baro spoke out on predestination in 1596 and crippled his chances of further promotion in the university, but John Overall, elected Regius Professor of Divinity in 1595, could not be silenced in his detestation of predestinarian views despite a major row in 1599. Indeed, proto-Arminians may have taken heart from the failure of the Lambeth Articles to gain official status in 1595; this was the first reverse suffered by the Calvinist ascendancy in the Church, a small portent of the near-complete rout of establishment Calvinism which Laud would captain under Charles I.[17] Yet if one considers the struggles of the Church of England in the 1630s, once more the paradox of English Arminianism becomes apparent: the chief battlegrounds became questions of liturgy and cere-mony rather than the debate about predestination and free will. As the Arminians emerged from the shadowy existence into which Calvinism had forced them during Elizabeth's reign, they took up with relish the *jure divino* themes pioneered by such polemicists as Bridges and Bancroft and made them their own; moreover, as an inevitable result of their vigorous assertion of the importance of the threefold ministry, they developed a sacramental theology which de-spite its novelty would have a permanent effect on the thinking of the English Church.

For many bitter opponents of such innovations in the early seventeenth century the source of it all was painfully clear: popery. There are in fact some indications that there was a grain of truth in this, and they link with Roman Catholic survival in the two universities. We have seen in Chapter 4 how Sir Christopher Hatton, the great patron of conformists from the late 1570s, had Catholic links including those from his Oxford days, and Dr Dent also suggests a continuity of personal links from crypto-papistry through to William Laud in Laud's beloved first home, St John's College, Oxford. Such links are particularly significant since up to 1606 Catholic recusants with patronage rights to benefices within the Church of England could exercise those rights as they pleased. Catholic gentry did not always play an active role in disposing of heretical patronage: for instance, that stalwart Catholic peer Lord Montague clearly found his Sussex patronage rights embarrassing and leased them out, often to militant Protestants. However, in East Anglia from the 1570s there are undeniable links of parish patronage, friendship and shared literary interests between various Cambridge dons and Cambridge-educated clergy of the established Church on the one hand and on the other, leaders of the East Anglian gentry Catholic community; the clergy concerned were marked out as enemies of Puritanism, and some had personal links with that doyen of anti-Puritan reaction, Archbishop Bancroft. One does not need to be a believer in conspiracy theory to seek further research into this intriguing sidelight on the reaction against Calvinism.[18]

Standing somewhat apart from the proto-Arminians was the Master of the Temple Church, Richard Hooker. Hooker was writing mainly for his own intellectual satisfaction, and only part of his great work the *Treatise on the Laws of Ecclesiastical Polity* was published in his lifetime. Nevertheless, he represents the most significant writer among Elizabethan churchmen in the long-term effect that his writings would have on the Church of England.[19] As the title of *Ecclesiastical Polity* indicates, Hooker's starting-point was not the soteriological debate of the proto-Arminians, but the attacks on the polity of the Church of England made by Presbyterian Puritans; this emerges immediately in the long preface addressed to Presbyterian sympathisers, which opens with a narrative of Calvin's proceedings at Geneva shaped in masterly fashion to Hooker's polemical purpose. The title of Hooker's book also reveals his central concern with law as the basis for church government. He rejected the Puritan attempt to discern patterns of church polity in scripture by maintaining that some essential features of Christianity such as the doctrine of the Trinity are not presented explicitly in scripture and need to be deduced by reason. This applied particularly to his chosen theme of church polity: reason is one aspect of three different types of law which interact to determine how a church should be structured. Law's threefold character consists of the law of reason or natural law, divine law and human law; it is the third of these forms of law, in England's case the law of the realm, which decides church polity in the light of reason and divine commands.

Hooker was no enthusiast for *jure divino* episcopacy; history may change the form of the Church and make another more appropriate to a new age. However, such changes do not invalidate older forms. Hooker was therefore quite prepared to admit that the medieval Church ruled from Rome was part of the true Church, instead of being an anti-Christian organisation which had oppressed and forced underground the only true Christians, as most English Protestants assumed, and this meant that the present-day Church of England could claim continuity with its pre-Reformation predecessor. Hooker was even ready to say that the contemporary Roman Church was part of the visible church despite its errors – this put him way beyond the most charitable of previous English Protestant writers. Suddenly the continuity which the Puritans deplored in the English Church was given a positive role: ceremonies were valuable precisely because they linked the past with the present. Moreover, in talking of ceremonies, Hooker demonstrated the clash over Puritan and conformist ideas of edification already discussed: for him, the ceremonies of an ordered liturgy and the systematic reading of scripture were means of edification just as much as preaching. Worship was the most important requirement in approaching God, rather than the exposition of God's Word from the pulpit, however much sermons might be the 'keys to the kingdom of heaven'; so a minister's function was just as much to pray as to preach. It was not surprising that with such preoccupations Hooker was led towards increasing emphasis on the sacrament of the eucharist and its central place in the scheme of salvation; there could be no better expression of his ideal of the Church as a worshipping community.

It will be obvious that Hooker was putting his commitment to reason to highly controversial uses, and giving reason a role which no Puritan could accept; he could and did appeal to Aristotle's analysis of the world as much as to the Word of God in scripture. One favourite theme of Hooker's which has assumed a leading role in Anglican thinking, the idea of the church of England as a *via media* between extremes of Christian thought and practice, is a reflection of Aristotelian ideas about the importance of moderation and the middle way. Equally significant for the future was a feature of Hooker's writings which he shared with the proto-Arminians, and which set him apart from such previous conformist writers as Whitgift quite as much as from Puritans: his apparent lack of interest in the great names of the Reformation. Apart from Hooker's account of the Genevan Reformation in the Preface to *Ecclesiastical Polity*, the whole enormous work cites Calvin only nine times, three times in order to disagree with him, and there is even less reference to other reformed continental divines; his whole approach, his insistence on deriving authority from a range of types of law, was alien to their concern with the commands of scripture.[20] While strikingly universal in his view of the past, Hooker became parochial in his view of the present: a retreat from the English Protestant internationalism which had seen its high point in Cranmer's Edwardian plans to bring together the whole spectrum of mainstream Reformation churches, and which was alive and well in the thinking of the Puritans.

This book has deliberately avoided the use of the term 'Anglicanism' in connection with the Tudor Church, because the distinctive and complex theological approach which Anglicanism represents can hardly be found until the proto-Arminians and Hooker had begun to have their effect on the Church of England's thinking. As Dr Lake points out, this makes it rather misguided to talk of Hooker as the defender of Anglicanism; Anglicanism did not exist before him, and it was his writings which contributed to the making of an Anglican synthesis.[21] A synthesis was essential because of the paradoxical nature of the Elizabethan Church settlement, with its peculiar arrested development in Protestant terms, and the ghost which it harboured of an older world of Catholic authority and devotional practice. Yet the attempt to tackle these contradictions of the English Church was only beginning to emerge in the conflicts and theological clashes of the 1590s.

From Hooker, classical Anglicanism has inherited its belief in the place of reason as an authority for action, its esteem for continuity over the divide of the Reformation, and a hospitality towards sacramental modes of thought. From the *jure divino* writers and the Arminians, it has inherited a theology of episcopacy and a penchant for splendid liturgy which would make the first generation of Elizabethan bishops look askance. From that first generation of the 1560s and the Puritans of later years, all doing their best to create a pure reformed church, it has inherited a contradictory impulse to assert the supremacy of scripture and preaching. The clashes between Calvinists and Arminians which would rip the Church of England apart in the seventeenth century were indecisive enough to leave Anglicanism unaligned with any one branch of the continental Reformation, yet also reluctant to accept the Arminian claims to represent the only authentic tradition in the Church of England. The seesaw battle between Catholic and Protestant within a single Anglican ecclesiastical structure has been proceeding ever since; yet for the Elizabethans, this battle was only just on the horizon.

7

REFORMING A MINISTRY

The creation of a reformed ministry was one of the great success stories of the Elizabethan Church: a success achieved in the face of the Church's lack of structural reform. In terms of formal organisation, *Ecclesia Anglicana* remained little more than a cut-down fragment of the pre-Reformation Western Church: the only significant move to improve administrative religious provision dated back to efforts made by Henry VIII in the early 1540s, creating new cathedrals and dioceses using buildings and some revenues from dissolved monastic houses. Only six were in fact erected out of a more ambitious list, although the usefulness even of this reduced scheme can be gauged by the fact that three of the old dioceses affected by the reorganisation (York, Lincoln and Coventry and Lichfield) had previously covered almost half the area of England, 14 other sees covering the rest.[1] Thereafter, major structural reform ceased and never gained lasting official momentum during the period covered by this book.

That part of Western Christendom which remained loyal to Rome was more structurally renewed than the Protestant Church of England by the end of the sixteenth century, and also retained a much greater variety of provision for ministry. In the old Church, provision for the liturgical round and for pastoral care and spiritual guidance from the clergy could come from a variety of sources: monks, friars and nuns, the diocesan and parish system, chantry foundations great and small. After 1547, all that was left in the Church of England was the system of diocese and parish, with the diocesan cathedrals having an increasingly isolated and anomalous role within a Protestant system which gave them little justification. Spiritual discipline continued to be exercised through courts which changed hardly at all in structure in the Reformation period, and were forced by circumstances to go on using the pre-Reformation code of ecclesiastical law right up to 1604.

Three problems must therefore be solved: how to provide effective leadership for the Church in an unreformed church structure, how to make a traditional system of church law serve the purposes of godly reformation, and how to create a ministry appropriate for a new task of spiritual care. Between 1540 and 1640, bishops struggled with a good measure of success to reassert their authority and restore stability after the confusion of mid-century; they also retained control over a system of court discipline which despite much radical Protestant criticism, achieved considerable and even growing results in enforcing its will on the population. Most crucially for the task of forwarding reformation, a combination of official effort from senior clergy and pressure from committed laypeople succeeded in turning a demoralised body of massing priests into a learned ministry capable of expounding the Protestant faith through the parishes of England and Wales. An irony whose exploration lies beyond the scope of this book is that by 1640, when this effort had achieved so much, a new political situation intervened to overturn a great part of the gains of a century.

Leadership and discipline

If we consider first the question of leadership within the Church, the picture is one of making the best of a bad job, of tinkering with a system in which the Crown prevented radical restructuring. There were plans aplenty for change.

It was obvious to anyone who tried to operate the system not only that dioceses were still too large, but also that the size of episcopal incomes and estates encouraged a bishop to play the role of a great territorial magnate, a species of clerical pretension which was precisely what Protestantism hoped to destroy. The Crown's pillaging of episcopal resources throughout the century from the 1530s did much to curb the bishops' wealth, but real superintendency would need much more drastic measures. John Knox, facing the prospect of a brave new world in 1558 amid the intellectual luxury of exile, had looked for a tenfold increase in English bishoprics; the radical thinker William Turner thought that four per shire would be a sensible rule of thumb, and a device offered to Parliament under Elizabeth capped that proposal by envisaging a total of 170 dioceses. However, it was significant how sincere Protestant leaders like John Jewel and John Aylmer abandoned such proposals for a new-look episcopate when as bishops they found themselves embroiled in the everyday task of running the church.[2]

If drastic change was not going to happen at diocesan level, could pastoral supervision be improved within the dioceses? Some suggested the appointment of *chorepiscopi* (assistant bishops), but in fact the number of assistant bishops within the English Church dwindled rather than increased during the sixteenth century; the help which medieval English diocesans had received from bishops with nominal titles derived from distant lands beyond the Church's control (*in partibus infidelium*) or from bishops with Irish dioceses (much the same thing in English eyes) came to an end, and Henry viii's creations of titles for suffragan (assistant) bishops had been reduced to one by the time of Elizabeth's death – John Sterne, Suffragan Bishop of Colchester, who died in 1608 and had no successor. Another possible source of help at much the same order of geographical size would be the network of archdeaconries, which often divided a diocese into two or more units more approximating in size to the reformed vision of pastoral care; indeed, archdeacons might take much of the work of promoting reformation off the bishop's shoulders if the two men could co-operate. However, archdeacons often had minds of their own which made their traditional role of 'the eye of the bishop' difficult to sustain, and their own time-honoured jurisdictions and interests might clash with the bishop rather than helping him. Some early Elizabethan bishops with unwieldy dioceses solved the problem of size by accepting the task as effectively impossible and acting as if they were bishop of a more sensible sized area: concentrating detailed attention on only that part of their diocese which happened to be within convenient striking distance of their home. Thus Thomas Bentham of Coventry and Lichfield supervised Staffordshire and Shropshire from Eccleshall Castle and John Parkhurst of Norwich the area around his one habitable palace at Ludham in Norfolk, and when John Aylmer of London was attempting to wheedle an additional Essex home out of the Crown in 1586, he claimed to have had a similar policy around his Hertfordshire residence.[3]

Yet another solution to the question of size might have been to exploit the potential of still smaller traditional units: many looked to the structure of rural deaneries to provide the right scale of supervision. In many dioceses before the Reformation, particularly in the north, rural deans were still performing a useful function, and this could have been expanded: the Puritan ecclesiastical lawyer John Becon saw the deaneries as the ideal unit for comprehensive reformation. Various bishops experimented with giving power and responsibility to the rural deans, notably Bentham at Coventry and Lichfield in the 1560s, yet such efforts quickly lapsed, and signs of an active and effective organisation of rural deans in the diocese of Worcester as late as 1603 are exceptional. Moreover, small units varying in size from a single parish to a group of parishes as large as a rural deanery might be 'peculiars' traditionally exempt from the bishop's control through some historical accident; although the bishops had secured a measure of control over such anomalous areas by legislation of 1540, old habits of independence died hard, and such peculiars were often notorious refuges for religious dissidence well into Elizabeth's reign.[4]

The English diocese was thus not a promising unit for pastoral reformation, and the episcopal system faced further problems which were largely of the Crown's making, as it pursued its assault on church estates in the interest of its own pocket and the pockets of a series of eager courtiers. Elizabeth kept several sees vacant for long periods. One of the motives may have been difficulty in finding suitable and willing bishops, since several of the dioceses concerned were in the north, presenting peculiar challenges of management, or were poorly endowed like Bristol, or in the case of Oxford and Ely, promised the headache of maintaining a good working relationship with Oxford and Cambridge universities. However, from the Crown's point of view, drawing the revenues of these vacant sees was a handy source of extra income, and the search for the right man may not have been too zealous. Even when a bishop was appointed, he faced the continual danger of losing further resources. The plundering of episcopal estates which Henry VIII had pioneered was institutionalised by the 1559 Act of Parliament empowering the Crown during any episcopal vacancy in a diocese to exchange the bishop's lands and other temporal possessions for spiritual revenues such as parish benefices, and a final halt to the nibbling away at episcopal estates was not called until legislation of the reign of James I.

The expectations laid on a bishop as a local figure of importance had not diminished in line with the dwindling of his resources; he still had his seat in the House of Lords like a secular peer, and was supposed to keep up a splendid household and dispense hospitality like his medieval predecessors. In addition, several early Elizabethan bishops faced financial disaster through accumulating taxation due to the Crown, which their own inexperience in managing a great corporation made all the worse; having already recorded the efforts of Parkhurst and Bentham to make the best of their situation, it is sad to have to note that they were foremost among victims of such troubles. Nevertheless, in the long run, the story is one of painful but steady recovery. Not all bishops were victims of their own holiness like Bentham or Parkhurst; many of them, a near-majority by the end of Elizabeth's reign, had served their management appren- ticeship as heads of those complex and frequently quarrel- some corporate bodies, Oxford and Cambridge colleges.[5] In the general tale of depredations on episcopal lands, there are some surprising anomalies, like the comparatively modest losses of the small but unusually wealthy diocese of Ely, or the evidence of royal forbearance on the wealth of the two archiepiscopal sees of Canterbury and York. Energetic and enterprising exploitation might produce rich dividends, as with Bishop John Still's gains from estate management and Mendips mineral resources in Bath and Wells at the end of the century.

One of the bishops' most serious property losses may actually have propelled them in the right direction in the long term: the wholesale Henrician and Edwardian confisca- tion of their London houses, which frequently meant embar- rassment at Parliament time – poor Parkhurst was once forced to rely on the offer of a London house from one of the leading Catholic recusants in his diocese, all the more galling because the house was unfurnished![6] However, the change was consistent with the shift of emphasis in the role of an English bishop to concentrate on his responsibility to his diocese; the significant contrast with the London spoliations is that of all the bishops' principal houses in their dioceses, only Bishopthorpe for York was lost (and that temporarily) by the end of the century. No longer did bishops find that their attention was taken by London duties, often in royal service; they were expected to be in their diocese, and the evidence is that very many of them assiduously used the opportunity of doing their duty as a Protestant superintendent by leading the diocesan work of preaching. By the last decade of the century they were also commonly adding to their episcopal employment by the revival of the rite of confirmation, a means by which, however hastily and amid great crowds, the ordinary churchgoer was brought into face to face contact, indeed literally in touch, with his father in God. This was an astute use of the bishop's liturgical store: small wonder that the same period saw bishops being hailed in a new light as the representatives of church authority *jure divino*.[7]

In establishing their authority in the reformed Elizabethan church, the bishops had at their disposal a complex traditional apparatus of discipline and communication. First, they had the right to call synods of clergy, for enforcement of decisions, administrative matters and discussion. Here the evidence suggests a good deal more activity than at the level of the rural deaneries, but still patchy: a lapse, for instance, in the diocese of Ely after the death of Bishop Cox, continuing existence in a modified form in the compact and well-administered archdeaconry of St Albans in the diocese of London, but a general picture throughout the dioceses of lessening activity. Of greater continuing importance was the allied process of regular visitation, where the clergy would be joined by the lay parish officers, the churchwardens, in being examined by the bishop or lesser officials within the dioceses. Here it is clear that bishops saw the usefulness of the system, and did their best to exploit it to the full: in the diocese of London, for instance, the evidence of slipping standards and casual attitudes to attendance at episcopal visitations in the 1560s is sharply reversed in the later decades of the century.[8]

In day to day terms, the church's authority at diocesan level would be diffused downwards through the ancient hierarchy of church courts in which it sought to wield discipline over the lives of everyone in the nation. How effective were these in practice? The study of church courts in the past has been bedevilled by an unfavourable and partisan view of them which was fuelled by the hostility of two highly articulate groups: common lawyers and Puritans. Common lawyers disliked the ecclesiastical courts because they operated under a rival system of law with its own traditions based on the international code of canon law built up by the medieval church. Henry viii had abolished the study of canon law, yet it remained the code which the church courts used, and the practitioners within the courts were still outside common law traditions and modes of training: civil lawyers, working according to international principles derived from Roman law. At many points the business of the church courts overlapped with that of the common law courts; in fact, throughout the century this overlap grew, since even before the Reformation upheaval, common lawyers were devising legal actions to try matters such as slander which had previously been the exclusive business of the Church, and since Acts of Parliament were increasingly dealing with matters of moral regulation, such as in the 1534 Statute against buggery. In a world where lawyers and rival courts within rival legal systems were chasing up litigation to earn their livings, there were therefore plenty of reasons for professional jealousy and rivalry.

Puritans were contemptuous of church courts because they were an obvious example of the unreformed structure of the English Church, and because their work of disciplining the population generally did not match up to the rigorous standards of discipline to which continental Protestant consistories in the Calvinist mode aspired; they did not contribute to 'edification', ignoring, for instance, calls for good scriptural penalties like death for adultery. Moreover, it was primarily the system of ecclesiastical law which was used to harass Puritan clergy and laity who expressed their disapproval of popish survival in the Church by various acts of non-conformity. The lawyers and officials who operated the courts were rarely sympathetic to Puritanism (John Becon, whom we have already mentioned, was a rare exception); after all, their primary job was to act as servants of the existing ecclesiastical machine, and they would hardly have a natural enthusiasm for attempts to overturn it. Indeed, well into Elizabeth's reign, many traditionalist ecclesiastical lawyers could barely conceal their hostility to Protestantism, their ostensible employer, let alone Puritanism.[9]

There were thus powerful vested interests for an unfavourable view of the performance of the church courts, paradoxically both because the courts were effective (thus raising the jealousy of common lawyers and the wrath of harassed Puritans), and because they were not effective enough for Puritan enthusiasts. Until recent years, historians have been inclined to take the hostile literary evidence created by these conflicts at face value without looking at the details of how the courts actually operated. Moreover, it was an unfortunate coincidence that one of the first historians properly to examine the detailed evidence, F. D. Price, was looking at an extreme case of an unsatisfactory church court system, that of the diocese of Gloucester: one of the new Henrician diocesan structures created from scratch, and set on a bad course from the opening decades of Elizabeth's reign by a Bishop with little administrative or managerial skill.[10]

Price's work appeared to confirm traditional pessimism, but subsequent studies have given a more encouraging picture. Certainly there were problems in mid-century, which were the result of the confusion and structural upheaval of those years. One important procedural casualty of this period was the widespread abandonment of suspending those appearing before courts from contact with a church if they were disobedient to the court's orders; suspension seems to have been an insufficient deterrent when the Church's religious unity had been shattered, and the courts increasingly resorted to the more drastic sanctions of the lesser and greater excommunication, the latter of which carried with it the threat of intervention from the secular authorities. However, from the 1570s, the courts' efficiency improved once more in step with the general recovery of nerve within the established Church, and a new generation of ecclesiastical officials were more wholehearted in their service to official Protestantism; the courts' business grew, peaking in the 1590s, and they achieved a very creditable degree of popular acceptance of their authority, as we will see in Chapter 8. The canon law under which they operated did not remain static until the comprehensive reform of 1604; flexibility in using it may have actually been encouraged by the fact that it was being operated primarily by practitioners from the civil law who brought other assumptions to bear on it.[11]

In the difficult years of the early part of Elizabeth's reign, the church courts were assisted by the intervention of the Crown using the royal supremacy to do justice in ecclesiastical matters by royal commission. There were precedents for such action dating back to Cromwell's exercise of the supremacy through his vice-gerency in the 1530s, and even Mary had used royal commissions to enforce her programme of Catholic restoration; Elizabeth used these powers of commission in a more systematic way, first creating a High Commission for each of the two provinces, and then appointing a series of diocesan commissions which gradually became permanent institutions. The major advantage of these commissions was that they could be staffed with religiously trustworthy and influential local laymen as well as clergy; gentlemen were less likely to be overawed by recalcitrant fellow-gentlemen; sorely-tried bishops trying to re-establish their authority in the 1560s might find it a relief to be able to back up their traditional jurisdictional powers with this symbol of royal power.[12]

The greatest years of effectiveness of the local commissions were in the 1570s, when the government was less afraid than in the previous decade of offending conservative local magnates, and used commissions to enforce an aggressive programme of eliminating traditional religious practice; in this period, the commissions were by far the most efficient way of curbing Roman Catholic recusancy among the gentry and substantial yeomanry. Thereafter, it seems to have been considered that the commissions had done their major work; their contribution to the fight against recusancy was superseded by purely secular recusancy commissions and by the secular courts after the recusancy legislation of the 1580s, and this was the time in which the regular apparatus of the church courts was once more performing with reasonable efficiency. Analysis of the membership of those diocesan commissions which continued to function shows in nearly all cases how the proportion of influential laymen sharply dropped from the 1580s. Professor Collinson is inclined to see the commissions as an experiment that failed, but it might be more charitable to see them as an effective response to an emergency, the mid-century crisis of traditional ecclesiastical discipline, which could be dispensed with when ordinary means could take their place.[13] The two provincial High Commissions remained in operation, with a power to fine and imprison which gave them considerably more sanctions than the rest of the ecclesiastical court system; the almost total loss of the records of the southern commission is a great barrier to understanding its workings, but its ruthless use by Archbishop Laud in the early seventeenth century showed rather too well how effective it could continue to be if used aggressively.

Creating a preaching ministry

The initial task was one of destruction: bringing down a system which lavishly provided the personnel for the needs of the old church, and which left to itself, would with little doubt have gone on doing so. Ordinations of clergy reached a peak in the 1510s and 1520s, but such levels of staffing would never again be achieved by the national Church. Over the next 30 years, numbers slumped in absolute terms, even within the parish system which did not suffer structural attack; this reflected a drastic fall in recruitment which must be an indication of shattered morale amid destructive change: who would wish to enter a profession which was no longer sure of the nature of its job-description? Both quantity and educational quality initially suffered. Even in southern dioceses where in the decades before the 1530s there had been a rise in the proportion of university graduates entering the priesthood, the number of graduates becoming beneficed clergy fell.[14]

Those chiefly affected by these substantial changes were

the clergy who had traditionally scraped together a living out of stipends in curacies, chantries or chaplaincies to fraternities, and who would rarely have hoped to move on to the next level of the clerical career by gaining a parish benefice. They were the lowest tier of what was in practice a three-tier system of staffing in the Church: stipendiary, parish priest and senior cleric. This 'clerical proletariat' might now have found job opportunities much reduced by the changes of the Reformation, as chantries and fraternities were swept away. Moreover, it faced competition from a host of former religious with a crying need to support themselves; most had pensions, but for various reasons perhaps as many as a third of the monks, friars and nuns ejected from their houses may have faced the world outside without any pension allotted to them, and we know little of their plight in later years.

Potentially here was a source of serious trouble for the government from a discontented group facing ruin. In fact, even with an influx of former monks onto the job market, the situation was not as desperate as it might have been: parliamentary legislation of 1529 limiting pluralities of benefice-holding to the wealthier livings gradually took effect in reducing the number of more modestly-endowed benefices held in plurality by one individual, and thus created more parish vacancies at a time when clerical recruitment had slumped: stipendiaries might now have an unprecedented chance to become beneficed clergy. One of the effects of the Reformation, therefore, was to transform a three-tier structure within the clerical career – humble stipendiaries, parish clergy, and senior clergy – to a two-tier structure of parish clergy and their superiors, which would be the basis on which the reformed Church of Elizabeth's reign would tackle the task of creating a ministry with a new direction.[15]

Efforts either to establish Protestantism under Edward VI or to revive Catholicism under Mary faced a Church whose staff consisted largely of an ageing band of mass-priests; neither the Edwardian nor the Marian regimes had enough time to do more than scratch the surface of the problem. Although a significant proportion of clergy took to marriage with enthusiasm under Edward, their depth of Protestant conviction in other respects was dubious; promising beginnings of Catholic clerical recovery under Mary were nipped in the bud by her death. The Elizabethan government could not dispense overnight with the services of thousands of clergy throughout the country, but it did its best to weed out the Catholic activists; it was significant that almost the first ecclesiastical act of Elizabeth was to muzzle the articulate minority of clergy by calling in all preaching licences. Generally, therefore, the Elizabethan changes in personnel meant purges among the higher clergy rather than the rank and file, although in some areas this could mean quite extensive action – for example, 41 deprivations of parish clergy in Sussex between 1559 and 1564, one in seven of all Sussex incumbents, and perhaps 300 throughout the country as a whole.[16]

For the first reformers and for a large proportion of their Elizabethan successors, the ideal would be for every church in the land to have provision for a sermon at all major acts of worship, and this was asking for a huge redirection of effort within the ministry. The emphasis would shift from a clergy whose prime duty was the faithful performance of the mass and the liturgical round to an obligation to handle abstract ideas and communicate them in a compelling form to the laity: not everyone would be naturally gifted like this, and for most, such skills required much more prolonged education and training than had been the norm for priests in the past. Medieval England had not been barren of clergy who were trained to communicate through the sermon: university graduates would be expected to preach, and the orders of friars had been created with the prime intention of presenting the faith in sermons. However, of the three tiers within the medieval ministry described above, graduates had largely been confined to the senior clergy and a minority of the incumbents of parishes. The Reformation had swept aside the orders of friars with their professional dedication to preaching: many of them, indeed, had abandoned their task of defending the traditional faith and had devoted their skills to promoting Protestantism. What would now be needed would be an expansion of the pool of university graduates whose training was some indication that they possessed the necessary skills.

At the outset this was quite impossible: removal of old clergy for traditionalist sympathies coupled with a high proportion of deaths in this ageing group meant an acute need for recruits which would take some years to satisfy. In the short term, while a new generation was training up in the universities, the Church authorities adopted expedients such as the ordination of older men, and even the authorisation of laypeople as 'lectors' or readers to provide the round of morning and evening prayer for parish churches without a clergyman; Archbishop Parker envisaged the lectors as a permanent order, but Edmund Grindal was not alone in detesting the experiment, and the idea lapsed for three centuries after the 1560s.[17] Instead, the strategy was to improve clergy quality to supply the parishes, and slowly and painfully this produced results; ecclesiastical documentation reveals evidence of a variety of individual diocesan initiatives to improve the quality of recruitment which are then mirrored in most dioceses in different decades. For instance, Ely records show evidence of careful discrimination in allowing men to go forward to ordination as early as the 1560s; not surprisingly, in dioceses further away from the natural recruiting centre of Cambridge university, such evidence comes from later years. The first effects of reforming energy were perceptible where supervision was most firmly based: in a drive against pluralism, the Archbishop of Canterbury's own Kentish diocese saw a rise in the number of beneficed incumbents from 153 in 1569 to 195 in 1575.[18] By the early seventeenth century, such improvements in the provision of pastors for the parishes would be commonplace throughout England.

In the 1570s, with the crisis of recruitment somewhat abated and the traditionalist party in terminal decline, the requirements for ordination were tightened up in important respects, one of the most significant moves coming in 1575, when it was laid down that prospective deacons must be at least 23 years of age and must serve a minimum of a year before proceeding to priest's orders. The effect of this, as Dr O'Day has pointed out, was to increase the attractiveness of investing in education before going forward for ordination. The medieval church had built up a system of minor orders below the diaconal order, which meant that one could start in lowly clerical functions at a much earlier age; these had been abolished by Henry VIII. Twenty-three was quite late to begin a new career, and since bishops were now insisting that manual labour was not suitable for prospective ministers, what was left to fill the intervening years but education, either as a student or a teacher? The new generation of ministers were therefore increasingly men with a university degree; again, the south was affected before the north, but by the 1620s, the church's leadership could look with satisfaction on a clergy almost entirely graduate in recruitment.[19]

From training the clerical elite only, the universities came to train virtually the entire ministry of the Church of England. This presented problems for the universities, whose classically-based curriculum was not an ideal preparation for pastoral ministry, and many colleges made efforts to supplement their courses for the benefit of potential ministers. The most ambitious attempt to make specific provision for clergy training in a university setting was the foundation of Emmanuel College, Cambridge, by the Puritan politician Sir Walter Mildmay: an interesting parallel to Cardinal Pole's plans for Catholic seminaries, or the realisation of those plans during Elizabeth's reign by English Roman Catholics in continental exile. Mildmay succeeded in providing a production centre for clergy who would arouse the suspicions of the Church's leadership; Emmanuel was a seedbed of Puritan disaffection well into the seventeenth century.

The success of Emmanuel highlighted the problem for Church leaders like Whitgift in the university expansion of clergy training: the Church's clergy were receiving their main preparation in institutions for the most part outside the Church hierarchy's control. After the break with Rome, the

Chancellors of Cambridge university were a succession of leading secular politicians, and Oxford did not get another clerical Chancellor until Archbishop Bancroft in 1608. Effective interference by the hierarchy at Oxford had to wait for an initiative from Archbishop Laud in 1636, and it was not surprising that until firm official Church control was established on a long-term basis at Oxford and Cambridge after the return of Charles II, the universities went on furnishing the Church with a large number of turbulent clergy. The Church did not succeed in providing an alternative training system outside the university setting for another two centuries; in Elizabeth's reign church leaders had to resign themselves to the unsatisfactory situation and wage guerrilla warfare with recalcitrant clergy through ecclesiastical discipline. Official energies in training at diocesan level were instead concentrated on the still serious problem of the unlearned clergy who were the relics of the mid-century confusions. Regular efforts were made to examine the learning of non-graduates, archdeacons being given official responsibility for such examinations in 1571 following *ad hoc* arrangements during the 1560s in certain dioceses, notably London. It was not surprising that Whitgift's confrontation with Puritan criticism of the status quo gave him a particular interest in promoting such activities, so from 1584 there was a flurry of activity throughout England.

These official drives met the sort of clerical resentment which has greeted post-ordination training schemes in every age, but they also aroused Puritan criticism for not going far enough. Puritan laity and clergy put their own efforts into improving matters. In the remote parish of Hinderclay in the heartland of Suffolk's radical Protestant tradition, the diocesan authorities of the 1570s were impressed to find that the parishioners had spent 20 years encouraging their unlearned parson to persevere with study; these humble folk were doing on a small scale what Sir Walter Mildmay was able to do for the clergy of the entire nation when he financed the foundation of Emmanuel. The 'prophesyings' of the 1560s and 1570s were also moves in this direction, and when

Elizabeth officially suppressed them in the Province of Canterbury, part of the aim of the clandestine Classical Movement of the 1570s and 1580s was to provide further opportunities for clerical training. The problem was to harness this enthusiasm to the purposes of the official church: Grindal's débâcle over the prophesyings demonstrated the difficulties, while a move in 1584 by Bishop Overton of Coventry and Lichfield to draw leading Puritan clergy into the examination of prospective candidates for benefices was peculiarly ill-timed in view of the nationwide battles over Puritanism, and it came to nothing.[20]

Part of the difficulty was that conformists and Puritans had different priorities in improving clerical quality: leaders like Whitgift wanted good pastors who could instruct their people through the official means provided. Sermons were essential, but due provision for them did not necessarily involve a barrage of freshly-crafted prose Sunday by Sunday; a regular diet of the official homilies was wholesome enough. Catechising, the instruction of both children and adults by set forms of question and answer summaries of official doctrine, should be the first concern. For Puritans, this was a wholly inadequate strategy: the need for preachers was paramount. Hence the widespread unofficial funding of new jobs for preachers ('lectureships') particularly in market towns, the natural local centres where people would gather from a range of communities over a wide area week by week. Many corporations made generous provision for such lecturers, who might, in a town like Ipswich with a number of ill-endowed parish churches, take on the role of a local religious superintendent; it is not surprising that such a clergyman, appointed outside the official parish system and with a formidable local power-base, should often be regarded with suspicion by the diocesan hierarchy, and during the early seventeenth century, the Laudian bishops provoked serious conflict with town lecturers.[21]

However, it was possible to provide a generous diet of regular preaching within the limits of the parish system through the device of lectures by combination: Professor

Collinson was the first to draw attention to the success of this idea, and it provides a good illustration of the way in which efforts to supply the need for preaching did not have to threaten the *status quo*. What the Church was doing was filling the gap caused by the suppression of the friars and their itinerant preaching. Bishop Barnes of Durham ordered in 1578 that all preachers in his diocese should make regular excursions to provide sermons, but normally it did not need official initiative to set up groups of beneficed clergy with preaching licences (or at least a locally-recognised ability to preach) to travel to provide sermons on a rota basis in a particular location: these were the basis of the lectures by combination or 'exercises', less luridly-named transformations of the prophesyings to which the Queen had taken such objection. Such lectures might happily coexist side by side with the service provided by a full-time stipendiary lecture; Collinson has been able to list surviving references to no less than 85 regular combination arrangements nationwide, and he has also corrected previous mistaken claims that the lecturers involved were unbeneficed clergy excluded from the regular ministry of the Church who constituted a potentially subversive group of 'alienated intellectuals'.[22]

The clergy of this Protestant Church had consciously repudiated much of the wonder-working character which had given medieval clergy their power: they denied that they performed a miracle in the mass, downplayed the role of individual confession and the absolution which could be conferred through it, and were for the most part profoundly suspicious of being credited with powers of exorcism. All this might have meant a diminution of status, particularly when the distinctiveness provided by clerical celibacy had also been rejected; yet for ordinary clergy, the loss of supernatural powers was to some extent compensated for by an unmistakable rise in social status. The effect of the various improvements perceptible among the English clergy by 1600 was, paradoxically, to create a new clericalism; if the medieval clergy had been separated from the laity by their wonder-working ability and their celibacy, the newly-married English clergy constituted a group with a recognisable professional status based on a common training, and increasingly demonstrated that consciousness by showing a marked tendency to marry within other clerical families.

Clergy group solidarity was probably encouraged by the fact that (as in the medieval period) few gentlemen came forward for ordination, and so gentle birth was rarely a rival source of identity for a clergyman. Instead, the English clergy embarked on the road to a status of sturdy-minded independence which has continued to characterise them at their best. Partly this was thanks to their new spiritual power over the conscience of those laity who willingly embraced godly discipline along Calvinist lines; Puritan ministers could be alarmingly frank in correcting the faults of their aristocratic patrons, and were often in return met with surprising meekness and compliance.[23] However, self-confidence was also backed by a relatively favourable financial situation. In general, the parish clergy's sources of income in tithe and glebeland had been little affected by the Reformation upheavals; if anything, agricultural price rises gave a boost to clerical resources. Through a combination of these factors, despite the crisis of clerical confidence and recruitment which lasted from the 1530s to the 1580s, a group of educated clergy, mainly preachers, first emerged as a select upper group among the older type of parish priest, and by the end of the century, had become the majority which set the tone for a self-confident clerical body with its own version of genteel respectability.

The story of cathedrals and their staffs can aptly be treated as a footnote to the main developments which we have traced. One of the great puzzles of the English Reformation is why the cathedrals survived as corporations without substantial alteration: it was here that the old devotional world cast its longest shadow for the future of Anglicanism. The cathedrals were based on a round of regular liturgy involving a large staff of clergy and emphasising elaborate music sung by paid professionals, all of which seemed to have little relevance in a Protestant church; nor did efforts to justify cathedrals by forcing their clergy into an active preaching role do much to alter their character. Part of the problem arose out of the cathedrals' traditional and little modified independence even of their bishops; effective control of cathedral corporations was exercised by a dean, and deaneries tended to be rewards for the great and the good who might have other more pressing priorities. Among numerous examples, one can single out Queen Mary's Secretary of State John Boxall, Dean of Ely, or the diplomat Nicholas Wotton, who achieved the rare distinction of being simultaneously Dean of Canterbury and York from the 1540s until his death in 1567. In comparison, the great civil lawyer Sir Thomas Smith could count himself ill-rewarded with the deanery of remote Carlisle, but then he had the handicap of not being ordained. Civil lawyers seem to have had a particular penchant for collecting deaneries, to judge by the (admittedly unsuccessful) efforts in 1588 of another layman, Sir Julius Caesar, to obtain the first deanery that might become vacant. Indeed, one of the reasons for the cathedrals' survival may have been precisely because they could act as a reservoir of patronage for the powerful to dispense to the deserving or the greedy.[24]

Lack of energetic supervision is at least one reason for the curious timelag in the pace of thoroughgoing reform perceptible in the majority of cathedrals: most retained a substantial body of conservative clergy into the 1570s, often in the case of cathedrals of Henry VIII's New Foundation, former monks of the monastic establishments which had gone before. Yet even after these had died off and been replaced by reliable Protestants, there was little drastic alteration in the cathedral ethos. Despite considerable strains of finance and organisation, the choirs went on singing, indeed forming a repertoire of new choral music which remains one of the chief glories of English artistic creativity. It is strange that this world of exquisite music, with a continuity broken only by the disaster of the seventeenth century Civil Wars, had virtually no effect on the musical and devotional life of the parish churches beyond the walls of the cathedral closes from the reign of Elizabeth down to the nineteenth century; yet that is not to say that it was without significance. The cathedral tradition came through the unpromising Elizabethan years to show the potential for liturgical splendour in the Book of Common Prayer; and that, as much as the theological shifts which we have examined in the previous two chapters, has been a major element in sustaining the religious power of Anglicanism.[25]

III

VOLUNTARY RELIGION

8

THE RECEPTION OF THE REFORMATION

Consent for change?

In recent years evidence has accumulated that there was plenty of health in the devotional patterns of the traditional Church on the eve of the English Reformation. Outward show may be thought to be a poor index to genuine piety, yet traditional devotion cherished the tangible as a doorway to the intangible. In this respect, the pre-Reformation English Church scored highly: England was noted by foreigners for its energy in lavishing money on church building and furnishings. How easily did the Reformation sweep aside such devotional patterns to impose new priorities? Was the Reformation a mere series of acts of state, pushed through regardless of the wishes of the English people? In the past, disagreements about this largely depended on the confessional bias of the historical commentator; but the cooling of passions about the Reformation has not ended controversy. Recent debate centring on the work of self-styled 'revisionist' historians has isolated two pairs of possibilities in describing the Reformation: rapid or slow? Imposed from above or rising from below?[1]

One reason for contrasting conclusions around the revisionists' questions is that the English response to the Reformation was fragmented by region: one area might indeed furnish data for a quick Reformation drawing on substantial support from below, another show a very late popular reaction to what successive Protestant regimes were attempting – 'slow and from above'. Surveying the large number of local studies of the Reformation undertaken over the last few decades, A. G. Dickens singles out as the area where the Reformation enjoyed genuine early popular support the 'great crescent' of south-east England stretching from Norwich to Hove, including East Anglia, London, and Kent and extending up the Thames Valley; beyond this there were outlying regions receptive to reform focusing on particular ancient urban centres such as Bristol, Gloucester or Coventry. Outside these areas in southern England, and through most of the highland zone north of a line from the Bristol Channel to the Humber estuary, there was much less enthusiasm for Protestantism, with a heartland of traditionalist survival in Lancashire which gives rise to the only major centre of Catholic activism with a popular base in late Elizabethan England.[2]

How can we explain these variants? One factor in acceptance of the Reformation was whether a region harboured a predisposition to reform produced by the survival of the medieval dissenting movement of Lollardy. There has been much disagreement about the effect of Lollardy on the course of the English Reformation, but in Chapter 5, we have already noted the way in which at the level of academic theology, Lollard preoccupations particularly coincided with the doctrinal concerns of the English reformers as those concerns moved further away from the initial influence of Luther and Germany towards the Swiss reform. At the level of popular religious practice, one cannot deny that there is a striking coincidence between the areas where Lollardy had been strong, such as East Anglia, the Thames Valley, the Chilterns and Kent, and Dickens's 'great crescent' of early popular Protestantism. From the 1520s, connections are well-documented between surviving Lollard groups and the underground organisations, such as the shadowy groups known as the 'Christian Brethren', bringing continental reformed literature into the country.

Another reason for variation was the strength or weakness of the parish system and its place in shaping the attitudes of local communities. The government's enforcement of the Reformation would have to prove itself effective at parish level; after all, the Reformation had set itself against the monastic life, so it could not use the alternative devotional structures of monasticism or the preaching task of the orders of friars. During the sixteenth century, the parish became a still more fundamental unit of national life, taking on an unprecedented role in local administration, as a series of Acts of Parliament gave more and more powers over poor relief to parish officers whose duties had previously been concentrated on the maintenance of the fabric of the parish church and the round of worship associated with it. If a government could effectively control what went on in the parishes, then it stood a good chance of imposing on the nation the will to religious change expressed in Acts of Parliament and in royal proclamations.

The problem for Catholic and Protestant alike was the uneven coverage of sixteenth century England within the parish network, still frozen through administrative inertia in the geographical pattern of the thirteenth century, and offering absurd anomalies 300 years on. In the lowland division of southern England it generally provided small, compact units – in Norfolk, for instance, whose nigh on 1000 parish churches and parochial chapels came near to equalling the entire parochial provision for Scotland. There were indeed anomalies, for instance in the Weald of Kent, where there were very large parishes, or in the fens of eastern England, now being reclaimed once more for much expanded settlement, but on the whole lowland England was provided with a parish system which offered the chance of detailed pastoral supervision either by a pre-Reformation parish priest or the Protestant minister who came after him. In the north of England, however, the situation was different. Some northern parishes consisted of largely empty uplands, as in the heights of the Pennines, Wales or the borders with Scotland, but not all northern monster parishes were barren wastes. Such a parish as Whalley (Lancashire), for instance, was in reality a totally different administrative animal from southern parishes, with its 40 townships and 16 places of worship embracing 180 square miles and a population of more than 10 000 – the parish priest here faced a potential workload equivalent to that of many an Italian bishop.[3]

For traditional religious patterns, this was not so serious. In the north, the deficiencies of the parish system might be compensated for by the continuing role of the monasteries, and gaps in northern pastoral provision might be up by chantry chapels which could stand as independent units, rather than as subordinate structures within an existing parish church building as was more commonly the case in the south. Pre-Reformation north and south were likely to have different patterns of devotional life, and the evidence suggests that this was indeed the case. In some areas of the south, the peak of traditional devotional practice as reflected in provision for furnishings and chantry foundations was past by the early sixteenth century. In East Anglia, the provisions made in wills and the architectural evidence of surviving church building indicate that the height of energy for providing devotional furniture came in the last three decades of the fifteenth century. From his work on the cosmopolitan and wealthy city of Bristol, Dr Burgess suggests that in a centre of very energetic devotional provision, the living found their obligations to the round of worship and to the welfare of the dead so burdensome that the Henrician government's attack on the old sacred world came as something of a relief. Other ancient cities and major chartered towns were experiencing severe economic difficulties and may also have found the round of civic ceremonial which was an integral part of their devotional life a heavy load to bear.[4]

However, in the north, the timetable of devotional change was different: in Lancashire, the movement to found chantries had taken off as late as the 1450s and was flourishing when Henry VIII's government snuffed it out. In Yorkshire, more chantries were being founded in the early sixteenth century than at any time since the early fourteenth; on both sides of the Pennines, the needs for pastoral care of the living through an extra supply of clergy may have been as important to founders as much as the needs of the dead. Not merely chantries were valued: the explosion of indignation at the closure of the monasteries in Lancashire, Yorkshire and Cumbria which was expressed in the Pilgrimage of Grace shows a depth of feeling about the importance and continuing relevance of monastic life which has been underestimated by many modern commentators on the risings and which found little echo in the south of England. Repression after the risings was fierce and that itself left a resentful groundswell of support for traditional forms of piety. To add to the problems of enforcing religious change amid the inadequate parish system of the north, the dissolution of chantries under Henry VIII and Edward VI weakened the provision of pastoral care: where there was pastoral need, chantry chapel buildings were supposed to be preserved, but in the overwhelming number of cases where the government's commissioners could prove that their endowments had 'superstitious' purposes, the chapels' source of financial support would be lost. The combination of these factors goes a long way to explaining why Protestant advance in northern England was so hesitant and patchy.[5]

We therefore need to bear in mind this contrast between highland and lowland when considering the 'above/below, rapid/slow' polarities. Naturally one should not be too determinist about the geographical divide. There were indeed strong early pockets of popular Protestantism in the north, for instance in the cloth-producing areas of Yorkshire and around Manchester and Kendal: places where industry and commercial movements of cloth encouraged contacts with the south. Moreover, no-one should underestimate the strength of Catholic resistance and survival in the lowland zone. After all, the compact, easily manageable parishes of southern England which offered the best opportunity for Protestant regimes to enforce their will had previously been the centre of vigorous Catholic lay piety; even if the height of this piety did lie in the fifteenth century, it could not be eliminated overnight.

Research on the localities has used two main sources to examine the impact of religious change: parish records, especially churchwardens' accounts, and wills. These tend to give two slightly different pictures. Parish records, as official documents, give an official version of local reaction: the response of parish officers to orders handed down from the government. They have the additional complication of interpretation that the surviving records are heavily weighted to the south and west of England, which makes it difficult to gain a clear picture of what was happening at parish level in the north. Wills reveal something more personal, the response of individuals facing up to the crisis of death; historians have paid particular attention to the religious preambles which were almost universal in this period to chart trends in traditional or reformed sympathies. Admittedly, one must recognise the limitations of this evidence: even wills are not purely spontaneous expressions of opinion. A testator was unlikely to make open financial provision for activities which a twist in government policy had made illegal, and the common custom of allowing the local clergyman or an experienced clerk to draw up the document might mean that the testator's religious views underwent some form of censorship, or were distorted by the personal preferences of the scribe. Nevertheless, combining these two varieties of source with more occasional, anecdotal evidence such as that provided by law cases in both secular and church courts, we can begin to build up a detailed picture of the reception of the English Reformation.[6]

Amid the uncertainties of the Henrician Reformation, parish officers seem to have reacted reasonably promptly to the necessity of dismantling the old religious furniture when told to, but rather less eagerly to the prospect of expenditure on new items such as an English Bible or the *Paraphrases* of Erasmus. The prime impact of religious change on them seems to have been negative: the destruction of old Catholic habits rather than the creation of Protestant ones – hardly surprisingly, in view of the ambiguities of what the government was doing. Ronald Hutton and Robert Whiting have shown how expenditure on church goods, ornaments and fabrics never regained former levels after 1540, and Whiting observes of surviving decoration in west country churches dateable to the 1530s, that there is already a move towards more secular or abstract subjects. Bequests to gilds in the west country began to decline significantly from 1536, and at the same time a new rash of lawsuits reflected growing disagreement about gild possessions and provisions for prayers for the dead.[7]

Already in the 1540s the old world was losing its enchantment. The preambles of wills confirm this, as a steady if gradual shift occurred from traditional formulae in which the testator bequeathed his or her soul not only to God but also to Our Lady and the holy company of heaven, towards formulae which may be more cautiously neutral or even Protestant in tone. Even in Yorkshire and Nottinghamshire, the traditional form of preamble began to disappear after the official condemnation of shrines and the cult of the saints in 1538. One needs to register the complexity of regional trends across the country: Kent, always in the vanguard of religious change, was quick to show the shift in formulae right from 1538, while Sussex did not begin to follow suit until the mid 1540s. Similarly there were striking differences between the archdeaconries of the very large diocese of Lincoln, with the archdeaconry of Huntingdon's marked reduction in the number of wills requesting intercessory prayers by 1545 contrasting simultaneously with a real and surprising increase in the archdeaconry of Buckingham.[8]

How much consent did Edwardian governments secure for the continuing programme of change? As in the 1530s and 1540s we can see from churchwardens' accounts that at least in the south, destructive change generally followed quickly on official orders, but that even here, positive provision for the new order came more slowly. No doubt this reflected widespread modified rapture about Protestantism: episcopal orders about non-attendance at church probably represent accurate perceptions that many people voted with their feet on the introduction of English services. Anecdotal evidence by the conservative Yorkshire priest Parkyn suggests that throughout Edward's reign, the north lagged behind the south in carrying out Protestant orders to alter ceremonies and purge church furnishings: and in remote Cumbria, it is probably symptomatic of conservative distaste for the spoliation of churches that unlike the parishes of southern counties, very few parishes sold their church plate before the Edwardian government began its official surveys with a view to confiscation. By contrast, in East Anglia, the Edwardian gentry establishment was embarrassed at the enthusiasm which a minority of radical Protestants showed in systematic destruction of rood screens, and tried to call a halt.[9]

Evidence in wills again indicates very different degrees of positive enthusiasm for Protestantism: at one extreme, a continuing rapid decline for traditionalist preambles in Edwardian Kent, with eight per cent of Kentish wills opting for a recognisably Protestant preamble formula by 1549, while in Suffolk, no less than 27 per cent of lay wills had Protestant preambles by Edward vi's reign. At the other extreme, before 1550 there are only two traceable Protestant will preambles out of nearly 900 early sixteenth century wills for the city of York, and only one in all south-west England.[10] Nevertheless, the Edwardian regimes only had to face one major rising which sought to restore the old religion, the Devon and Cornwall rising of 1549, and even here other motives may well have been equally important. Above all, here was a conservative rebellion which never mentioned the Pope in its published list of demands: one of the twin pillars of traditional Catholicism evidently meant little in the west. The risings of eastern and south-east England in 1549 reveal more enthusiasm for Protestant changes than traditional religion, and no evidence of the gentry involvement which the Courtenay connection created in the western rebellion; gentry conservatives anxious to embarrass Somerset's government looked to them in vain. It was also significant that the north had been sufficiently cowed by the repression following the Pilgrimage of Grace a decade before to offer no serious challenge to the Edwardian changes.[11]

Mary's regime faced a task both of undoing negative work from the previous reign and of building up positive enthusiasm for Catholicism. To rebuild the formal devotional life of the parish churches was the easiest part of the task, although it required a formidable amount of detailed and energetic supervision; in many parts, particularly in the north, the old Latin services were restored with spontaneous enthusiasm. Even in Kent, the most recalcitrant part of the country, and that which had been most closely under the eye of Cranmer's administration, the work of restoration of Catholic church furnishings was satisfactorily advanced in four-fifths of the parishes after four years, and this was exceptionally slow; otherwise, once more hardpressed churchwardens hastened to follow the latest whim of government. An essential accompaniment to this restoration was to refashion the role of the clergy by restoring celibacy, leading to the largest upheaval in clerical personnel of the century as about 2000 married parish clergy in England and Wales lost their livings. This was a necessary clearing of the ground for renewal of lay piety, although since many of these clergy proved supple enough in conscience to regain livings elsewhere by forswearing their wives, it was unlikely that they would be promising material for reinvigorating traditional church life.

Gradually, the rise in the number of traditionalist will preambles registered the slow rebuilding of Catholic practice, at least among the predominantly middle-aged and elderly who were likely to make wills: in Yorkshire, conservative recovery began to accelerate after a couple of years. Yet in the time available, the recovery could not be complete, and was swiftly reversed on Elizabeth's accession.[12] For many, the credibility of the old structure of prayer must have been shattered when the mass had been silenced and monasteries and chantries closed without the Last Judgement arriving or the sky falling in. From his exhaustive search of Marian parish accounts, Dr Hutton concludes that the cult of the saints and provision for souls in purgatory were 'abiding casualties' of the work of Edwardian destruction. Even the gilds, formerly the vital outlets for popular lay piety, were not restored in any significant number, and many of the ones that were restored seem to have been little more than fund-raising bodies. A few new chantries were founded as proof of the energy of the newly visible Catholic party among the local elites, but the only monasteries and friaries to be set up anew were primarily the result of the Queen's initiative: there are few traces of enthusiasm for this effort of restoration among people at large.[13]

On the other side of the religious divide, one cannot ignore the evidence of continuing Protestant vigour in the face of apparent disaster, which was particularly provided by the number of Marian martyrs. Moreover, the tally of actual martyrs is a minimum figure, distorting the map of Protestant survival: the overwhelming concentration of martyrs with residence in Sussex, the Home Counties, London, and East Anglia largely reflects the enthusiasm of the persecuting classes there, both clergy and gentry. The lists of those who went into exile compiled by Miss Garrett reveal a wider picture, although the bulk of those who left were gentry; a substantial body of Protestant gentry left from the south-west and Lancashire and Yorkshire, showing that the conservatism of the north and west was beginning to dissipate among those people most likely to have a national perspective which would balance their remoteness from the Protestant heartland in the south-east.[14]

Wills give a more comprehensive picture of the distribution of resistance to Catholic restoration, by the number of preambles which either defiantly retain Protestant phraseology or show dumb insolence to Catholicism by adopting some neutral form of commending the testator's soul to God. Even in a sample of Yorkshire wills, A. G. Dickens could find a quarter falling into these categories during Mary's reign, and among the laity of Marian Suffolk, the combined figure for both categories was as much as 52 per cent, with 16 per cent continuing to use explicitly Protestant formulae; the figure for Protestant preambles in Sussex was still ten per cent by 1557. This was a daunting block of opinion to have to redirect, and in the short time available, not much could be done. In some respects the impact of the Protestant approach to religion could never be shaken off: for instance, Bible-reading could never be relegated to the side-lines again. It is significant that Mary made no moves to withdraw the English Bible, and equally telling to find that staunch supporter of the old ways, the Yorkshire parson Robert Parkyn, urging Bible-reading as part of his rule for the Christian life.[15]

Accepting a new order

We noted in Chapter 2 that among the clergy, aristocracy and gentry, the Marian reaction drew the demarcation line between Catholic and Protestant more sharply. Through the population as a whole, the government was faced with a nation where popular conservatism was deeply entrenched in the north and west, while popular Protestantism, battered but largely unbowed, retained strength in the south-east; yet these opposed groups probably represented minorities. The rest were probably punch-drunk on religious change, passively wedded to traditional habits and shapes of life, but largely apathetic to either extreme of religious activism. The task of the Elizabethan Church would be to extend consent beyond this apathy, preferably to turn the whole nation into Protestant activists. The measure of success was considerable, although there remained a minority of committed Roman Catholics and a small group of Protestant sectaries for whom the encouragement to activism had been only too successful; those two groups of outsiders are the concern of Chapter 9.

Once more, as with the Edwardian and Marian ventures, the first task must be destruction: to remove once and for all the structures and habits of devotion which helped Catholicism retain a sway even among the religiously apathetic. This meant altering even the shape of the sacred year, albeit in a partial and cautious way: the work of reformation was not nearly as thoroughgoing as Puritans would have liked. The structure of feast and fast days remained, although simplified, with a continued official expectation that people would attend church on Wednesdays and Fridays as well as Sundays and feast-days. The dilemmas posed by the partial nature of change were reflected in the treatment of the one major piece of public ceremonial to gain continued official backing: the parish Rogationtide processions. These could be justified because of their importance in preserving the exact memory of parish boundaries, but their association with popish processions was a dangerous one, quite apart from the copious drinking which might accompany them. The royal Injunctions of 1559 sought to end their popular role by ordering that only 'substantial' parishioners should take part, and similarly, one can note one Elizabethan bishop of the first generation, Thomas Bentham of Coventry and Lichfield, doing his best in 1561 to hedge them round with further anxious restrictions: no crosses, tapers, rosaries or women allowed.[16]

The full co-operation of the authorities at local level would be needed to ensure that a Protestant liturgical year was not unduly tainted with popish survival. The progress of this effort was an index of the gradual replacement throughout the country of conservative gentry, borough leadership groups and parish officers who would hold back the process of change: a process which in Chapter 3 we saw begin to take effect even in the far north during the 1570s, after the defeat of the northern rebellion. A case in point was the suppression of community drama: in the first aggressive phase of the Reformation, Protestants had used plays to convey their message, but this impulse faded with the establishment of the Elizabethan Church. From 1559, very little official Protestant religious drama was encouraged, although a contrary development was the gradual popularising of celebrations of

Elizabeth's accession day; meanwhile the authorities waged a steady war of attrition on the plays which had been one of the most effective means of reinforcing medieval Catholic doctrine. The bulk of these had been suppressed by the end of the 1570s, each suppression a new mark of the steady loss of control by local conservative elites who had persisted in defending them; by the end of the century, the rich fund of medieval religious drama was lying dormant in manuscripts to await later rediscovery.[17]

As the governing elite was brought under increasingly effective control, it would be easier to influence the religious habits of the population at large beyond the suppression of such semi-official activities as processions and plays. This would involve dealing with the survival of personal habits of piety like the use of rosary beads, and a constant effort to eliminate these by official prosecution in church and secular courts. Throughout the 1560s open traditionalism persisted throughout England and Wales, in supposedly Protestant lowlands as well as reactionary highlands: for instance, a formidable variety of Catholic practice reported in the diocese of Chichester in 1568, or problems in Norwich diocese in suppressing bell-ringing for All Hallows in 1569.[18] In most parts of the country during the next decade, the loss of elite support for any new generation of traditionalists among more humble folk meant that much of this religious deviance could be dealt with by that great church worker, Death, as the aged took their habits of piety with them to the grave.

A partial exception lay in the north, in the unusual conditions of Lancashire: here the same reports of widespread traditionalist practice continue to the end of the sixteenth century. However, the exceptional nature of the situation in Lancashire is underlined by the government's unusual experiment in appointing four Queen's Preachers to spread the Protestant message in the county in 1599; another significant sign of Lancashire's difference is that as late as 1598 the ecclesiastical commission of Chester diocese (which included much of Lancashire) was remodelled to include a

large number of laity to strengthen its disciplinary effectiveness, at a time when most other diocesan commissions had
done their work and so ceased to function, or had reduced
their activities and had lost gentry membership. Lancashire's
neighbouring region of Cumbria seems to have been as
resistant to attempts to keep Catholicism alive as it was to
Protestant activisn and the same is true in the uplands of
Northumberland. Lancashire also contrasts with the other
side of the Pennines in Yorkshire, where in the same period,
the ecclesiastical authorities had a considerable degree of
success in containing Catholic survival both among the
gentry and the population at large; probably they were
helped by the presence of the Archbishop and the Council of
the North at York, lending muscle to the attack on
Catholicism.[19]

Wales (so far entirely neglected in my Anglocentric study)
might seem to be as unpromising an area for the reception of
Protestantism as Lancashire; certainly in the early stages of
the English Reformation, it showed virtually no trace of
interest in reformed ideas, and the Edwardian government
had not done much to encourage any. As a result, reports of
the most outrageous traditionalist survivals are commonplace from Elizabethan Wales; yet the long-term success of
initiatives here by the Elizabethan church authorities is in
stark contrast to the dismal English record in presenting the
Reformation to the inhabitants of Ireland. Braving continuing English prejudice against Welshmen, the Welsh
gained a useful foothold within the English university world
with the founding of Jesus College, Oxford, in 1571, and
leading figures within the Elizabethan Church showed a
sympathetic understanding of the peculiar challenges posed
by a region with a distinctive language and culture. Despite
notorious and continuing deficiencies of pastoral provision
among the whole body of Welsh clergy, it was a great
advantage in tackling the religious challenge of Wales that 13
out of 16 Elizabethan Welsh bishops were native Welshmen,
and among these it was William Morgan of St Asaph who
made the decisive move which would win mainstream Welsh

culture to Protestantism: the translation of the Bible into good literary Welsh. At a time when the Welsh bardic tradition was in decline, apologists for official Protestantism provided a lifeline for the survival of the language: it would be the deficiencies of a later age in the established Church which would squander its early success.[20]

The work of transformation was thus remarkably effective across the nation: naturally it was not complete. Some fragments of the old world took their cue from the survival in modified form of the liturgical year, adopted new guises and found a home within the reformed Protestant parish. Thus bell-ringing survived Puritan disapproval to transform itself from an act of piety into a national sport; it is no coincidence that the only evidence of widespread and large-scale activity in church building in the later sixteenth century relates to improvements in church towers and recasting of bells, necessitated by the introduction about 1570 of new technology in bell-frames which revolutionised the possibilities of change-ringing. The English liking for an elaborate celebration of death also survived reformed suspicion that such extravagance reflected hankerings after purgatory: the monstrous tombs of Elizabethan gentry often house gentlefolk of impeccable Puritan credentials, and Puritans also came to abandon their dislike of the panegyric funeral sermon, the oral equivalent of these majestic structures, to turn it into a favourite rallying-point for the godly. It is also noticeable that the traditional medieval habit of only communicating once a year, usually at Easter, widely persisted despite the official requirements that the minimum should be three times: here conservatism probably combined with church officials' horror at the cost of providing wine for the entire parish more than once a year to produce a silent consensus in modifying official liturgical practice.[21]

Other fragments of the past community life, like games, dances or popular feast-day celebrations, were unable to achieve respectability in new clothes, particularly where local magistrates were strongly Puritan in character; often they were associated with Sundays, and this offended against the strong sabbatarian conviction general through both continental and British reformed Christianity that the only proper use of Sunday was to approach the throne of grace in worship and in the hearing of sermons. In order to survive, such pastimes would increasingly be forced to part company with the timetable of the godly in the parish church and seek refuge in the alehouse, a growing phenomenon of the later sixteenth century. When in later generations Archbishop Laud tried to encourage their return to parish life in a revival of church ales, the godly saw this as an attack on the fabric of English society. The reordering of English religion was in danger of creating two worlds: one sanctified, the other religiously indifferent.

How far this separation of two worlds became a reality will be considered in Chapter 10, but we should assess the 'revisionist' thesis of Christopher Haigh that one consequence of the restructuring of English society on Protestant lines was a growth in anti-clericalism, a phenomenon which has conventionally been seen as more characteristic of the laity before the English Reformation than after it. Haigh points to the sporadic nature of public agitation against clerical pretensions before the Reformation, and claims that in any case, the amount of clerical misconduct was not great enough to arouse lay hostility: surviving anti-clerical literature reflects grievances of particular laypeople against particular great clerics like Cardinal Wolsey, or of particular small interest groups like common lawyers and merchants. He also cites evidence of difficulties for the post-Reformation Church courts in enforcing their will, which he suggests shows a growing contempt for their authority, and he argues that the more professional clerical grouping of the Elizabethan church may have been more likely to arouse anti-clerical feelings than its medieval predecessor.[22]

Haigh scores some palpable hits in arguing that pre-Reformation anti-clericalism has been exaggerated, although he underestimates not only the English literary corpus on the theme built up since the fourteenth century and extended by the early English Protestant reformers, but also the evidence of disputes between pre-Reformation clergy and laity over such matters as tithe, particularly in London. However, he is less convincing in arguing for a new Reformation anti-clericalism; it is perhaps significant that the only evidence which he quotes for such popular feeling comes from the heartland of robust traditionalism in Lancashire, that notoriously individual area of Elizabethan England. One powerful piece of evidence pointing in the other direction is the continuing effectiveness of the church courts after the undoubted crisis of authority which they faced in the confusions of mid-century: even Haigh somewhat paradoxically admits the greatly increased volume of litigation which these courts experienced through the century, a rising consumer demand which presumably reflects consumer satisfaction.

The situation of the courts and their significance for assessing the success of the reception of the Protestant Reformation is seen in a number of recent detailed studies of the sources, but most notably in the work of Martin Ingram. Ingram examines previous claims of high rates of non-attendance at and defiance of church courts, and finds that many of them do not represent a norm. Many statistics showing low appearance rates for accused relate to occasional visitations over wide areas, the least likely to encourage compliance; smaller jurisdictions even in the north of England could be markedly and increasingly more efficient, an instance being an attendance figure of 80 per cent in the archdeaconry of Cleveland by 1634. The lowest figure which Ingram can find for his home ground in the archdeaconry of Wiltshire is 65 per cent for 1602. Moreover, recalcitrance was dependent on circumstance; it was much commoner in disciplinary or 'mere office' cases brought by the authorities than it was in the very considerable volume of cases between party and party, where both sides were likely to have an interest in turning up – secular courts had the same problem. Recalcitrance was at its highest in discipline cases involving sexual offenders, which were likely to concern the most undisciplined section of society, the young and unmarried; and if their non-appearance in court represented actual flight from the community where their offence had been committed, many might see this as a highly satisfactory result of the case rather than a failure on the part of the courts.[23]

Ingram's picture of the Protestant church courts is of institutions which managed to command widespread consent, and not just among the Puritan busybodies of their day. A remarkable instance of this is the way in which they reflect a victory for the Church in the reformation of marriage discipline, admittedly a victory in a struggle which had concerned the medieval Church as much as its Protestant successor. Hesitantly and at different times in different places depending on the strength of residual regional conservatism, the late sixteenth century Church succeeded in destroying the ancient custom of espousal before church wedding; from 1580 the courts were taking notice of ante-nuptial incontinence which would previously have been considered as justified within espousal custom, and correspondingly there was a rise in the proportion and number of church weddings. This was not imposed on an unwilling population, but went hand in hand with increasingly widespread strictness in sexual morality. Perhaps this was as much to do with economic stress as with the impact of Puritan attitudes, but the effects of this late sixteenth century shift can be seen in the falling bastardy rates of the early seventeenth century.[24]

There are other instances of the church courts' continuing perceived social usefulness, for instance in the service that they gave to victims of slander; they acted as agents of community harmony in an age where this was a state of affairs much prized, and when the disappearance of the institution of regular confession to a priest had removed one ancient safety-valve for parishioners' bad feeling. The courts' concern to regulate sexual morality chimed in with the desires of most people, and meant that even if many resented their constant busyness in social engineering, they could rely on widespread continuing popular co-operation. In later years, the courts were defeated precisely because they had relied on consent; Laud's encouragement of a change in the direction of their activities was already endangering that consent before the outbreak of the civil wars. After this disaster for the Anglican system precipitated by the Archbishop's policies, the courts returned in 1660, but the persistence of Protestant non-conformity on an appreciable scale meant that the old consent was never again forthcoming.

9
PRINCIPLED DISSENT

Roman Catholicism

Principled dissent to the Elizabethan Settlement came from two directions: Catholic and radical Protestant. Of the two, it was the Roman Catholic menace which seemed the more important and which the government and the Church spent more time combatting. After all, throughout the reign, the section of the population whose sympathies lay with loyalty to Rome included many of the peerage (perhaps as many as a third as late as the 1580s) and a sizeable section of the gentry, while in the exceptional case of Lancashire there may have been more Catholics than Protestants in the population at large at the death of Elizabeth: as late as the seventeenth century in the Fylde, the Catholic heartland of Lancashire, there were probably still more Catholic clergy than clergy of the established Church.[1] Yet the story of Roman Catholicism amid the 1559 Settlement of religion is one of failure: failure to recapture the nation or bring about alteration in the state of the Church of England.

The initial problem for Catholics was that the traditional Church had always been firmly based on a structure of received authority, particularly clerical authority: in 1559 a purge of significant conservative clergy was undertaken (see Chapter 7) and the Marian bishops vanished from sight once they had made their initial stand against the government,

144

ending their days in house arrest of varying degrees of comfort. Over the next few years the remaining Catholic intelligentsia in the two universities left for continental exile, just as the Protestants had done under Mary. The ordinary clergy of traditionalist views were accustomed to take orders from above, and were in no position to fill the vacuum of leadership. The burden would therefore fall on the leaders of the countryside, the nobility and gentry. Even the most enthusiastic gentry supporters of the old order took a decade to make the decisive break with the new establishment, giving it a vital period to consolidate, and the rebellion sponsored by Catholic aristocrats in the far north in 1569 proved a dismal failure. It was doubly unfortunate for Catholics that in 1570 the Pope issued a Bull, *Regnans in Excelsis*, condemning Elizabeth as a heretic and absolving her subjects from their allegiance to her. The Bull had been intended to help the northern rebels, but it was not issued and advertised in England until after they had been defeated. It provided a hideous new embarrassment for Catholics instead of helping them: how could they dodge the question of whether their loyalty was to the Queen or to the Pope? Even the issuing of an 'explanation' of the bull by the Pope in 1580 saying that things being as they were, Catholics were not bound by the bull until it could be publicly executed, did not alter the fact that the practice of Catholicism offered a public challenge to the Elizabethan government.

This challenge might not have seemed too serious if Catholicism had remained the faith of a minority of the middle-aged and elderly. As the Henrician and Marian priests who sustained traditionalist religious practice grew more elderly and then died off, English Catholicism might wither away with them for lack of clerical support. This did not happen, however, thanks to the work of the exiles who had fled to the continent. One of them in particular, William Allen, a former Oxford don, founded a college at Douai in Flanders as an act of private enterprise. This would train a new breed of cleric who would remedy the faults both of the old conservative church and of the Protestant Elizabethan

Settlement; Allen was a true son of the Counter-Reformation which was transforming the Roman Church. In the early 1570s, Allen came increasingly under the influence of the most dynamic expression of the Counter-Reformation, the Society of Jesus, and it was the Jesuits' intense spirituality which would characterise the students of Douai from the middle years of the decade. The first missionary priest arrived in England in 1574, and with him died the government's hope of a slow unspectacular death for English Catholicism: the sort of death which Catholicism was undergoing in mainland Scotland or Scandinavia.

The 1570s and 1580s, the decades which saw a determined campaign to destroy the new arrivals, began an age of heroism for the Catholic community in England which has formed the backbone of their hagiographical writing ever since; however, by the 1590s tensions were developing in the Catholic community which the arrival of the seminary priests and the consequent repression had newly defined. Part of the problems lay in rivalry between the Jesuits and the other clergy who were seculars, that is not members of a religious Order: disagreements became particularly acute when priests were confined together in English prisons or in almost as close quarters in continental training colleges. The problem was partly the lack of any overriding authority in the shape of a bishop; indeed attempts at such provision became part of the problem after 1598 in the tangles of the 'Archpriest Controversy'. Secular priests, both surviving old clergy and secular seminarists, were often suspicious of the dominant role of the Jesuits, but there were also differences in outlook about missionary strategy and the question of where a Catholic's loyalty should lie. Should Catholics obey Queen or Pope? The Jesuits followed the principle of their founder and insisted that every Catholic should first obey the Pope; they also insisted that the Catholic community should keep itself completely separate from the Church of the Elizabethan Settlement. A party among the secular priests blamed the Jesuits for the severity of government persecution, and hoped that if the Jesuits left England, they could gain some sort of toleration; from their appeal to Rome against the authority of the Jesuit-dominated Archpriest George Blackwell, they became known as the Appellants.[2]

The government was naturally delighted at this division and encouraged it, even if there was no serious intention in government circles of allowing toleration. Few people of whatever mainstream Church could then conceive of a state which contained more than one Church, and this was in effect what the seculars were proposing. A government proclamation of 1602 made it clear that the most that would be offered was personal protection against the treason laws for those priests who repudiated the doctrine that the papal power could depose an English monarch; it did not give them freedom to practice their priestly office. Only 13 secular priests took up the offer; yet the concession which they were making to the state was precisely the sort of compromise that the bulk of the Catholic laity had been making with the Elizabethan government throughout the reign. Even if it was the first very cautious step towards the toleration of more than one religious group within the English state, for the time being it only served to intensify the quarrels of the Catholic community.

The contentions among the Elizabethan Catholic clergy have been reflected in recent years in a controversy about who should enjoy the chief credit for building a Catholic community, and what the nature of that community was: survival or a revival? Continuity or discontinuity? John Bossy based his magisterial survey of English Catholicism on the proposition that a Catholic community was newly created by the Jesuits and other seminary-trained missionaries out of an amorphous mass of traditionalist sympathy within the established Elizabethan Church: uncompromisingly he states 'in the beginning was the Church of England'.[3] This extreme version of a line much favoured by the seminarists in the sixteenth century has been strongly contested in recent years, most aggressively by Christopher Haigh, who sees the formation of a separate Catholic community identity as being primarily a product of survival: the perpetuation of existing patterns of practice and thought, sustained by surviving clergy from the past who would not become absorbed into the new Protestant establishment, and owing little to the strategy and assumptions of the Council of Trent. Indeed, Haigh still further mirrors the tensions between all seminarists and the Catholic clergy surviving from before 1558 by taking a cool view of the strategy and missionary commitment of the seminarist effort.[4]

Undoubtedly there is much force in the arguments for continuity; after all, the initial acts of recusancy in 1568 predated the arrival of the seminarians (see Chapter 3, n. 12). The Catholic community's links with the past are most obvious in Haigh's special case of Lancashire, where the large number of old clergy who made the most tenuous of concessions to Protestant change and strongly-entrenched popular conservatism made it possible for Catholicism to continue something like the regular parish activity of the past. However, the case is not merely made on special pleading from the Lancashire example: what is noticeable elsewhere is the vital importance for later Catholic survival of Elizabethan gentry who had strong links with senior pre-Reformation clergy, particularly if these clergy were relatives. Such links can be shown in areas as diverse as East Anglia and Northumberland to be of great significance in deciding who among the gentry would take the road of Catholic recusancy after 1568.[5]

Nevertheless it is important to realise the limitations of this approach. Marian clergy could be a two-edged blessing for Catholicism: although many acted as a conservative fifth column by their persistent and ambiguous presence within the Church of the 1559 Settlement, that presence may have encouraged many conservative laity to feel that they could have a place in the new Protestant church order, and to become reconciled to it by degrees. The old clergy might be particularly weak in fostering one element which would be essential for the creation of a distinct Catholic community: loyalty to Rome. The old system of devotion had been based before 1533 on two pillars, traditional religious practice and the central position of the papacy; Henry VIII had succeeded in eliminating any widespread sense of papal loyalty even among committed religious conservatives, and the shocks of Mary's reign had only begun to rebuild this sense. Rebuilding papal obedience alongside traditional devotion was one item on the Tridentine agenda which may have been the particular contribution of the clergy trained on the continent; it remains to be demonstrated that enthusiasm for papalism would have emerged from the traditionalist clergy on their own.

Proponents of the survivalist case have also got to explain why some areas of conservative survival did not give birth to strong Catholicism: north-west Wales, Cumbria or Cornwall, for example. Survivalism alone cannot account for later Catholic geography. In East Anglia, for example, one can note survival of yeoman religious conservatism in particular areas into the 1580s, and there are signs that these areas correlate with those which before the Reformation had large, strong gilds drawing their membership from several parishes; yet these potential yeomen Catholics, drawing on a tradition of especially vigorous lay devotional practice, had no successors.[6] Through most of England and Wales, Catholicism survived in dependency on gentry sustaining Catholic clergy who were, inevitably, increasingly the product of the seminaries; otherwise tendencies might not find the resources to become a sense of separate identity. One might then agree with Dr Haigh in criticising the seminarists for relying on the gentry so much and for concentrating on the easier pastures of the south-east rather than both nurturing the more numerous faithful in the north and developing the potential of more farflung areas of survivalist traditionalism. However, given the centralisation of power in early modern England (unusual for a state of that time), one can defend the missionary strategy: the gentry generally and the gentry of the south-east in particular were the centre of initiative in English political life, and without hindsight, it might make good sense to put effort into such bases.

It can hardly be denied that by the end of Elizabeth's reign this strategy had failed in the task of reconverting England: the Catholic community was increasingly introverted and cut off from the mainstream of English political life. The Catholic community had refused to follow the call by militants among the Jesuits, particularly the brilliant schemer and writer Robert Persons, to become a dynamic force in winning souls: the indecisive outcome of the clerical disputes of the 1590s and 1600s was the measure of this refusal, and the resulting story of Elizabethan Catholicism was, in John Bossy's phrase, 'inertia to inertia in three generations'.[7] Why was this? First, even in its revived state, Catholicism was only one extreme band on a religious spectrum, with the Protestant sectaries at the other end. Among the laity many gentry of a conservative persuasion were content to stand on the edge of the community, becoming what were known as church papists: the head of the household would continue to attend Protestant services to preserve the family estates from ruinous fines by the government, while his wife remained a Catholic recusant and he turned a blind eye to what went on in the household. Although Puritan clergy and Jesuit missionaries fiercely condemned this practice, it suited a good many people, and has even been seen as the salvation of English Catholicism; yet it contained the constant danger of haemorrhage towards the established Church, and was not likely to breed aggressive Catholic attitudes.

Second, the nature of the Catholic community's leadership was significant: as already noted, the pattern of Catholic survival common by 1603 was of a scatter of gentry households across a county, each surrounded by communities of dependent humble folk who kept to the old faith. A Catholic group of yeomen or of the 'middle sort' hardly existed, since they were the most vulnerable to the fines for non-churchgoing which the gentry were better able to sustain and which the government did not bother to collect from the very poor. The only significant exception to this rule, the region with a more representative cross-section of the population, was Lancashire.[8] There could be advantages in relying on the gentry. Many of them were so intricately linked to other families by marriage that family organisation alone could be a means of ferrying priests secretly round the country. Also as Elizabeth's reign wore on, Catholic families tended to marry into Catholic families, so the community became ever more identifiable and distinct from its Protestant neighbours.

However, gentry leadership might do as much to blur Catholic identity as to create it. Many Catholic families continued to have close Protestant relatives, perhaps even a brother or sister. Among the older generation of gentry, many might feel considerable affection for the parish churches where their ancestors were buried and which often their family had taken the lead in building; even after 1558, some of them seem to have been more interested than their Protestant gentry neighbours in building extensions to or making benefactions to churches.[9] Few Catholic gentry ever forgot that they were English gentlemen: most of them were quite fervently and genuinely loyal to Queen Elizabeth, and felt that this loyalty was more important than the squabbles of a collection of priests which became such an unhappy feature of the Catholic community during the 1590s. The seminary priest was the product of a sort of spiritual black market – a commodity increasingly unobtainable in any other fashion – but for many gentry, once obtained, he was a household amenity rather than the spiritual director and popular missionary which he might wish to become.

Moderation among the Catholic community was encouraged by continuing lines of communication with heretics. Many gentlemen had friends at Court as well as locally, and it is clear from the beginning of the reign that the government were not prepared to wipe out Catholic gentry who were not causing trouble. The government did not even want to beggar the recusant gentry: a Catholic who was a pauper and in prison was a man with nothing more to lose, and therefore ready to adopt desperate measures, while a reasonably well-to-do Catholic was an easy source of income. Few paid the full fines which the law demanded, but some paid substantial sums which came in very handy for hard-pressed royal finances; others got off scot-free through their various contacts. From the 1590s, persecuted gentry and government persecuting machine seem usually to have settled down to a rather surprising degree of symbiosis. Elizabethan government was a very untidy world, and astute Catholics could benefit from that untidiness when they chose.[10]

All this amounted, therefore, to repression much tempered by muddle and unexpected tolerance. There were heroes and saints among the Catholic priests and gentry; there were also incidents which can only be described as comic. Few Catholics were prepared to follow desperate courses to further the Faith after the desperate courses of 1569 had failed so dismally. The various assassination plots on Elizabeth's life and the Gunpowder Plot of 1605 were entirely untypical of English Catholics, and even among the exiled clergy, the advocacy of political resistance was confined quite narrowly to the period from around 1584 to 1595, years when English Catholic writers could draw much inspiration from the short-lived political militancy of the Catholic national *Ligue* in France.[11] Being largely dependent on the gentry, priests were powerless to conduct large-scale missionary work when they failed to convince the Catholic gentry that it would be a good thing. Immense sacrifices were made to preserve Catholicism, and it was necessary to make those sacrifices, for the government was out to destroy Catholicism even if it was not out to destroy Catholics. Nevertheless, English Catholicism became fossilised for almost two centuries as a largely upper-class sect with a faintly exotic flavour, before its great nineteenth century expansion.

The Protestant dissenters

In many essentials, the aims of Reformation Christians were the same as those of the medieval Western Christianity which they sought to destroy: to worship a triune God, to win salvation and also, ever since the Emperor Constantine I had begun the alliance between government and the Church in the fourth century, to mould the whole of society into a shape which could be considered agreeable to God. Both sides talked of the Christian God in terms thrashed out over five centuries of argument in the early Church, culminating in the theological juggling of the Council of Chalcedon in 451; both sides looked to the same scriptures to justify their particular road to salvation, and both sides assumed that the whole nation was entrusted to them for pastoral care and guidance on the way to eternal life.

This was the faith of mainstream Protestantism: the 'magisterial Reformation'. Only small groups of radical Protestants came up with any variations on it, and as a consequence they were hated and feared by Catholics and mainstream Protestants alike. The word 'Anabaptist' which was commonly associated with these radicals was one which struck terror in the minds of all those entrusted with authority, particularly after the nightmare of the seizure of the German city of Münster in 1534–5, bloodily recaptured by a combination of Catholics and Lutherans; the fact that most Anabaptists both before and after Münster were emphatic in their rejection of any form of violence did not reduce fears that another Münster was waiting in the wings. Indeed, there are signs that one of the ploys which the Elizabethan regime used to unite the country's conservative and Protestant local leaders in the delicate opening months of the new reign was to set them looking for Anabaptists.[12]

The search would usually have been in vain. Despite early contacts with the radical groups of the continental Reformation, radical religion in Tudor England proved to be a rare phenomenon embracing small groups, possibly because the established Church Settlement of 1559 (rather against the will of many of its leaders) proved remarkably flexible in playing host to a wide variety of lay activism. We have already alluded to the spectrum of Tudor religion which makes it so difficult to draw exact confessional boundaries, and if this is true of the traditionalist minority, it is even more of a

problem with Protestant religious activity. A useful set of
distinctions which is an aid to sorting out the confusion is that
adopted for instance by David Loades: non-conformity,
separatism and sectarianism.[13] Non-conformity is a tendency
to defy religious uniformity while remaining more or less
within the bounds of the established church; it is important
to distinguish this use of the word from the later formal and
denominational use of 'Nonconformist', which in Elizabethan terms would imply a separatist. A separatist rejects
the mainstream assumption that the Church should include
everyone, in favour of forming self-selected 'gathered' churches of the godly; while sectarianism may go further in
challenging the basic doctrinal statements of Chalcedonian
Christianity, in a variety of different and often incompatible
ways. Nevertheless, when making these distinctions, we
should always be aware of the compelling power of the idea
of Christendom, the overarching Christian society expressed
in a universal structural Church: this meant that the most
apparently sectarian groups might produce surprising links
with the establishment.

Before all else were the Lollards, whom all shades of
Protestant opinion claimed as part of their genealogy: where
do they fit in the threefold analysis? Recent research on
centres of Lollard activity as widely separated as Colchester,
Coventry and the Buckinghamshire parish of Amersham has
revealed far more people of substantial wealth among the
Lollards than had been previously realised: the sort of
people of 'the middling sort' who could become parish
officers and indeed did so despite their Lollard sympathies.
Sometimes one can find evidence of gatherings which suggest a regular separated church group, but Lollards were as
much 'occasional conformists' as the church papists of Elizabethan England, and the evidence of most official examinations of those who were caught by the pre-
Reformation Church shows that their doctrines, based on
their treasured fourteenth and fifteenth century texts, were
firmly within Chalcedonian orthodoxy.[14]

The Lollards, then, look like non-conformists, or at most

separatists; yet they sheltered a number of people with eccentric religious beliefs, and also provided a climate for scepticism about received truth which for some might prove fertile ground for new and more corrosive ideas. From the 1520s a variety of continental influences from both the magisterial and radical reformation movements began to construct an English Protestant identity; yet the orthodoxy of English Protestantism could not possibly contain all the imported theological wares on offer. Anabaptists, as their name ('rebaptisers') implies, rejected the value of baptism from the existing churches and practised the baptism only of consenting adults; some of them further denied the reality of the Trinity, either from rationalist motives or because their fundamentalist reading of scripture could not find the doctrine in the sacred text, and so turned to some version of Unitarian belief.

From the 1530s hundreds and perhaps even thousands of these varied sectaries fled to England from severe continental persecution, only to meet fresh persecution and a number of executions of immigrants by the English government. However, radicals were soon aware that English persecution was not sustained or systematic; the coming of a Protestant regime under Edward vi encouraged the influx of refugees, and an alarming variety of belief was allowed to come into the open when Somerset's government repealed the heresy laws. The mainstream Protestant reformers now felt compelled to suppress this by a fresh round of repression, including the burning of a native Unitarian sectary, Joan Bocher, in 1550: a later embarrassment to John Foxe, who could not admit her to his Book of Martyrs.

Edward vi's reign saw at least two variants of sectarian radicalism in England, and the links between them are not obvious. First there was the persistance of a very broad and amorphous grouping of Anabaptists, who went on into Elizabeth's reign to boast six martyrs executed by the government between 1575 and 1589. One small variant Anabaptist group which emerged in Edward's reign was to have puzzling success in England while it died away on the continent;

a group known as the Family of Love. Its founder was a German, Hendrik Niklaes (usually known by his followers by the initials H.N.), who may have joined the Dutch section of the London Strangers' Church under Edward: Niklaes sent out travelling preachers who were particularly successful in Mary's reign in recruiting East Anglian Protestants disorientated by government suppression of the official Reformation. For the rest of the century and down to the Civil Wars, groups of Familists persisted in the eastern counties; with encouragement from their founder to indulge in systematic deception, they showed a genius for publicity in somewhat contradictory combination with a secrecy which makes it very difficult for us to gauge just how numerous they were. They sparked off a notable wave of government alarm between 1575 and 1580 when it was discovered that some members of the Queen's personal guard were Familists, and recent research reveals that in particular communities they persisted as respectable and substantial citizens, even undertaking such paradoxical public duties as that of churchwarden: a pattern oddly reminiscent of the Lollards before them. Mainstream Puritans loathed them, and the great clerical leader of Suffolk Puritanism John Knewstub was able to lessen his disagreements with the church hierarchy by becoming an acknowledged expert in combatting the sect.[15]

The other Edwardian radical sectary group had curiously little effect in the future: the Freewillers, a disparate collection of people from clergy to the unlearned humble, based in Kent and Essex. As their name suggests, this grouping went against the whole trend of the official Reformation and also against the inclinations of most Elizabethan radicals in resisting predestinarian theology to proclaim the value of human free will and decision on the road to salvation: they championed free discussion, emphasised the importance of individual devotion, and it was not in their nature to set up formal church structures. Although they survived Edwardian harassment to argue with scandalised mainstream Protestants in the midst of common Marian misfortune, they vanished from the scene thereafter, leaving no published literature and no traceable links either to the wave of academic Arminianism which was to confront predestinarian theology at the end of the century, or to a new emergence of free will views in the separatist John Smyth. How they relate to the Anabaptists and Familists who shared their base in south-eastern England is not clear, and altogether the group continues to present an intriguing puzzle.[16]

The repression of Protestantism under Mary gave encouragement to the alternative radical impulses of nonconformity and separatism. Mainstream Protestants who had concurred with Catholics in the previous reign in persecuting radical religion now found themselves persecuted alongside the sectaries and like them, having to improvise secret organisation in order to survive. This caused some interesting confusions among Marian Protestants. Clandestine groups in London may have received help from Protestant exiles in setting up their organisation, and adopted a church structure which although apparently Genevan in form did not inhibit two of its clerical leadership (Thomas Bentham and Edmund Scambler) from becoming bishops in later years. Nevertheless, in such emergency conditions, discipline from the official Edwardian leadership would be hard to maintain, and one commentator (admittedly a hostile Catholic) noted the leader of a secret congregation in Islington denouncing Cranmer and Ridley as well as Mary's church. Elsewhere the Marian persecution swept in sectary martyrs who would cause John Foxe further problems when he came to write them up in the later years.[17]

Even when Elizabeth restored a version of true godliness, many of those who had been steadfast enough to worship separately under Mary might feel little enthusiasm for a return to the establishment. The first evidence for their presence comes from the group unearthed by Bishop Grindal of London in 1567, worshipping in secret in Plumbers' Hall. They had followed some ministers who had been dismissed from their official livings in London by the Bishop during the Vestiarian controversy, and cherished their continuity with secret Protestant congregations under Mary; one or two of them had been Marian exiles, and were merely doing what they had done then by choosing to worship in their own way in defiance of authority (see Chapter 3). Over the next few years there were probably four or five such congregations ('conventicles') within the capital. In East Anglia too, as late as the 1580s, heroes of the Marian underground were prominent in the formation of groups of the godly recruiting over a wide scatter of parishes.[18]

Such congregations as these were unlikely to be separatist by conviction, and indeed in a myriad ways they would retain links with the untidier loose ends of the established Church. In London, for instance, the peculiar or extra-parochial jurisdiction formed by the site of the former nunnery of the Minories had links with these gathered congregations at the same time as affording a haven for non-conforming Puritan ministers, and peculiars everywhere gave a chance to evade the uniformity which the church authorities wanted to impose. In the north of England, the attempt to enforce uniformity against Puritanism was much less stringent, and it is probably as a result of this that separatist conventicles were much rarer and later in developing than in the southern province. In the south, where the church hierarchy was more aggressive in confronting Protestant non-conformity, what might develop was what Professor Collinson has called 'an idiosyncratic congregationalism', linked to the round of parochial public worship through the sermon. A good sermon might draw radical enthusiasts for Protestantism to public worship, although admittedly this might mean ignoring the parish system; in East Anglia, some Elizabethan 'sermon-gadders' refused to go to services according to the Book of Common Prayer, but might travel four or five miles to hear a parish minister who was known to be a good preacher. One of the important practices of informal Protestant devotion was to repeat sermons heard in church, and by this means even a private meeting of the gathered godly might remain tied to public worship.[19]

This untidiness reflected a general tension in the thought of the 'magisterial' reformers between their desire for their churches to encompass all society and their awareness that only a minority might respond with positive enthusiasm to the reformed message: hence the emergence in many reformed Churches of groups which in effect were gatherings of the consciously godly alongside the mainstream of the congregation. Various English parishes with forceful Puritan-minded incumbents ended up showing this sort of division, with the administration of communion restricted to those who showed themselves worthy; the social divisions which this 'social separatism' revealed were, in an extreme case, fossilised in certain parishes of Kent and Northamptonshire during the 1580s and 1590s by the practice of giving the children of Puritan families made-up didactic names such as 'Repent' or 'Bethankful'. One can indeed argue that this social separatism was more disruptive to the harmony of a community than a decision to withdraw altogether from public worship. Full separatism into private gathered congregations was thus one logical outcome for that Reformation search for unspotted religion which in England was chiefly seen in Puritan thought; yet it remained only one in a spectrum of solutions to the problem of gathering the godly in fellowship.[20]

Full separatism emerged in the early 1580s, and virtually all the significant leaders were Cambridge dons with a radical Puritan background. The most well-known, Robert Browne, is also the least constant in his views – an unstable, violent character who ended his days as a conformist clergyman – yet he came to symbolise the movement to the extent that separatists were habitually labelled as 'Brownists'. Driven from a turbulent Puritan ministry within the established Church by the indifference of his parish congregation to his message, he founded his first separatist congregation at Norwich in 1581, and soon his activities, like those of many Elizabethan separatists, were transferred to exile in the safer territory of the Netherlands. Here in 1582 he regrouped a little flock and issued two books justifying his stance, the first being the celebrated *Treatise of Reformation without tarrying for any*. This title showed how he had left behind the confused attitude of mainstream Puritans to the established Church of England.[21] An unhappy characteristic of these early groups was their quarrelsomeness, and Browne and his Cambridge friend and fellow-exile Robert Harrison soon went their separate ways, each taking supporters with them. A mark of how seriously the government took their deviance from the ecclesiastical norm was the persecution which separatist leaders then had to suffer: there were at least three and possibly five executions during the 1580s, with another three leading figures (Henry Barrow, John Greenwood and John Penry) during the flurry of repression in 1593.[22] Separatists were as much to be kept at bay as heretical Anabaptist sectaries, although they died for sedition rather than heresy. After the wave of arrests and imprisonments which at the end of the 1580s left sectaries and mainstream Puritans alike in considerable disarray, a fresh initiative came from Francis Johnson, another Cambridge don, who in 1591 made the same journey as Browne from radical non-conformist Puritanism to thoroughgoing separatism. Taking refuge in Amsterdam to avoid government persecution, his congregation remained tiny and once more riven with quarrels, but one of the schisms which took place within it was of great significance for the future shape of English Protestantism.

One of Johnson's most enthusiastic followers was yet another young Cambridge academic, John Smyth, who by 1607 had made the by now familiar transition through Puritanism to leadership of a Lincolnshire separatist congregation organised on the lines of Johnson's Amsterdam group; however, once in Amsterdam, at some time in 1608 or early 1609 he decided that he must signal a new beginning for the Church by rebaptising himself and then a group of his followers. The shock for Johnson was grievous, and this and a series of unconnected misfortunes resulted in the gradual disintegration of the congregation which he had founded. Smyth parted company still further from Johnson by embracing quasi-Arminian views: when churches with a settled separate identity emerged after the British civil wars, it was Smyth's congregation which was claimed by the

General (that is, Arminian, non-Calvinist) Baptists as their source of origin.

English separatism had thus produced beliefs about free will and believers' baptism which look remarkably similar to the views of Edwardian and later sectaries, and it is not surprising that historians have argued for a strong Anabaptist connection for Smyth's ideas, particularly since Smyth ended his personal spiritual pilgrimage in a Dutch Anabaptist congregation of Mennonites. Positive evidence for contact between English separatists and sectaries is hard to find, and their mutual detestation would make such links unlikely. Moreover, one does not need to look for such connections to account for Smyth's distinctive views: one need only consider the covenant theology which we have seen emerge as such a characteristic feature of mainstream Puritanism, and note within it the possibility of arguments about unconditional or conditional covenants of God (see Chapter 6). Separatists were particularly fond of the covenant idea, which gave them an ideal way of structuring their gathered congregations of believers; yet they might use conditional and unconditional covenant rhetoric in different ways. In defending infant baptism against Anabaptists, even infant baptism administered by the corrupt established Church, they used a standard argument of the magisterial reformers by drawing an analogy with Jewish infant circumcision, a sign of the unconditional covenant of God to Israel. However, both Puritans and separatists increasingly emphasised the conditional nature of the covenant, an emphasis which would undercut this whole approach and predispose Smyth's thinking to believers' baptism; Puritan arguments from the conditional covenant might also lead to quasi-Arminian views about salvation without any contribution from anti-Puritan 'proto-Arminian' intellectuals such as we have described in Chapter 6.[23]

Once more we may use John Bossy's phrase 'in the beginning was the Church of England'. The groups of sectaries which had no truck with magisterial Protestantism from the start survived in various obscure forms into the confusions of the British Civil Wars to link with fresh manifestations of sectarian impulses, but the English Free Churches take their origin not from the sectaries but from those fragments of mainstream religion which the established Church failed to contain, and whose non-conformity was thus driven further into the shape of separatism. The process of complete separation was slow. The separatist leader Henry Jacob, whose establishment of a congregation in Southwark in 1616 has often been seen as the true ancestor of English congregationalism, was perfectly willing that his gathered congregations should be convened in synods by the magistrate; he had no radical notion of separating church and state.[24] The final separation was as much a result of seventeenth century Anglicanism creating an increasingly narrow identity for church establishment as it was a conscious theological decision on the part of separatists.

10

CONCLUSION: A WORLD BEYOND?

By 1600 a Protestant Church in England had succeeded in marginalising significant principled dissent both from Catholics loyal to Rome and from other Protestants. Yet how far could the new establishment claim to play a central part in the lives of the whole population? Was there, as historians of the Reformation and Counter-Reformation like Jean Delumeau have suggested, a significant stratum of society which remained largely unaffected by religious practice both before and after the Reformation? Did the standards of religious comprehension and literacy which were demanded by Protestantism, the religion of the Book, exclude a good proportion of the population, and did magic and witchcraft play a more central part in the lives of many people?[1]

At the time there was much pessimism about the popular effectiveness of evangelisation: gloomy guesses at the proportion of those truly transformed in their lives, such as the despairing estimate of one-fortieth of the population in 1572, or the unimpressive improvement to one-twentieth of the population 'Christian indeed' suggested by a writer of 1617; the Essex Puritan parson George Gifford acutely if sadly observed the prevalence of 'low-temperature' religious observance which he styled 'Country Divinity'. Yet much of this talk was a combination of unrealistically high expectations of what should be achieved and a tendency natural to Calvinists to think in terms of small minorities of the elect stranded in a mass of the unregenerate: sometimes the gloom may have concealed pious relish.[2] Part of the problem must lie in the greater priority which Protestantism placed on literacy for religious understanding: the literate person was likely to be more capable of absorbing abstract religious ideas, particularly the intractable arguments contained in Paul's Epistles which were so central to the Protestant religious revolution, and the literate person was going to be more easily able to listen to expositions of Christianity in sermons and turn to personal Bible-reading. Moreover, the ability to write was a significant indication of membership of articulate society. The undoubted improvements which took place in the numbers of those able to write during the sixteenth century were markedly biased towards the powerful and prosperous; they left the labouring class and a growing number of vagrants, between them perhaps a quarter or a third of the population, nearly as illiterate at the end of the seventeenth century (at around 80 or 90 per cent) as they had been at the beginning of the sixteenth.

One has to be cautious about the significance of these statistics: they measure the ability to write, but the ability to read was more important for the absorption of Protestantism, and it was an easier skill to acquire than writing; a person who could read could also influence a much wider group by reading to them aloud, and there is good evidence that this was particularly important in the early stages of establishing popular Protestantism. Nevertheless, the connection between literacy and Protestantism was a serious handicap for Protestant evangelism in a society where the proportion of male illiterates varied between a half and three-quarters depending on area, with a distinct skewing of literacy towards towns and and their hinterlands; illiteracy figures for Tudor women may have been as high as 90 per cent.[3] Protestantism thus had a particular challenge in the rural areas which throughout England we have seen as generally most tenacious of religious conservative practice, but everywhere it had a difficult task in reaching the very poor. It is not surprising that modern commentators have linked these problems to contemporary evangelistic pessimism, and pictured a society divided between a consciously godly and literate minority and a greater number of what the Puritan ministers of the Dedham *classis* referred to as 'froward poor men ... every way disordered'; moreover, the increase in vagrancy during the century would have presented an obvious problem for any settled system of pastoral care.

The detailed work of Keith Wrightson and David Levine on the Essex village of Terling has been particularly influential in providing a concrete example of such a polarised community. Widespread social changes encouraged such 'social discontinuity': for instance, the repewing of churches, given an impetus by the Protestant emphasis on the sermon; there is abundant evidence of physical social segregation within churches, as pews ranked in social order were constructed and church finances began increasingly to depend on revenues from renting out pew space to those who could pay. Outside the church building, it is tempting to find the heart of opposition to good order and Protestant advance in the proliferation of alehouses which is such a marked feature of the sixteenth century. Alehouses had played a significant role in spreading Protestant ideas in the early days of the Reformation while the Protestant faith could still be seen as new and potentially subversive, but Protestantism in the days of its establishment showed little gratitude for this early hospitality, and did its best to suppress them.[4]

Nevertheless, we need to be cautious about the 'social discontinuity' thesis. Undoubtedly there were Terling-style divided communities, but Martin Ingram's contrasting findings from villages in Wiltshire suggests that they may not have been typical: conditions in the Puritan heartland of Essex may have been unusually favourable for creating a self-conscious godly elite. Conversely, Margaret Spufford has suggested that such patterns of internal conflict between law-abiding substantial people and the 'froward' can be traced as far back as the thirteenth century, and therefore have little to do with the coming of Protestantism. What seems more plausible than a class of people systematically and throughout their lives staying away from church in favour of the anarchic pleasures of the alehouse, is the existence of an alternative culture of the young: a culture certainly not fully under the control of the godly and respectable, but which was half-tolerated because it generally came to an end with the coming of apprenticeship or marriage. Dr Ingram and Professor Collinson agree in identifying a youthful, unmarried and unusually mobile group of the population which was less amenable to restraint; although alehouses were not exclusively patronised by the young, people under the age of 25 formed a high proportion of the population, and would be a particularly significant part of the alehouse clientele.[5]

The presence of unruly youth in the alehouse was reason enough for those in authority to be suspicious of such places and take especial care to regulate them in time of social strain; moreover, gentry antipathy towards the world of the alehouse was not just a Puritan characteristic. It was true that the alehouse was a social institution more sympathetic to traditional values and pleasures than to Puritan social regulation, but the alehouse could not exactly preserve the old world of communal leisure activity. Traditional games and plays had involved the whole community from high to low, but the alehouse was a haven for the lower orders away from their social superiors, and there was little hierarchy in its jollifications; this might make it a source of suspicion to the most devoted gentry patron of good old customs and of Merrie England. The alehouse seemed to threaten all good rule, although in practice it rarely fulfilled upper-class fears perhaps because such a high proportion of its clientele was always haemorrhaging towards middle-aged respectability: Dr Clark describes it as 'less in the van than in the baggage train of an alternative society'.[6]

However much one modifies the idea of social discontinuity, the gap between the growing literate group and the humble illiterates is a fact; yet both official and unofficial energies were devoted to bridging it. The English Reformation was not as skilled at using pictures to convey its message as Martin Luther had been, but there were considerable efforts to produce devotional prints purged of popery which could be stuck on the walls of taverns or humble homes; in particular, the pictures of Foxe's *Acts and Monuments* proved a lasting success for English Protestantism. Educational effort was also spent in providing catechisms: if people were not capable of concentrating on a sermon, the supervised rote learning of the catechism might be more use. Apart from the catechism provided in the Book of Common Prayer, which many considered too short to be effective, there were a host of attempts to do better which reveal increasing expertise in producing works simple and clear in style and targetted towards specific audiences. By 1600 a population of around four million was furnished with perhaps half a million copies of officially authorised catechisms and three-quarters of a million unofficial rivals: an impressive achievement which is the index of a heroic effort of religious instruction by clergy and godly laity alike.[7]

Another aspect of the 'world beyond' was the popular belief in magic, the supernatural and witchcraft. The campaign to reduce the power of magical belief was a real problem for the new Protestant establishment, more so than for the medieval Church: traditional religion had its own powerful magic of the sacraments, in the miracle of the mass, the dissolution of sins in absolution, and direct confrontation with evil powers in exorcism, so its quarrel with alternative magic systems was not so much about whether they were true as where the control of the supernatural should properly lie. Protestants were intent on destroying Catholic claims to supernatural power in ordinary people's minds, and their fight against popery was often closely linked with their determination to suppress superstitious practices of all descriptions; they were inclined to treat popular magical belief with the same rationalist contempt in which they held the miracle of the mass. Often their hostility to the claims of magic put them at a disadvantage in the fight against popery;

surviving Catholic priests and new seminarists were much more prepared than most Protestant ministers to demonstrate their continuing miraculous powers of healing and exorcism. There were indeed Protestant exorcists, but generally Calvinist theological presuppositions rebelled against the idea that God's majesty could be manipulated by the petty conjuring of human beings. Equally sceptical was the small minority of intellectuals interested in the ancient ideas of neo-Platonism, who rejected the claims of popular magic because of their belief in more comprehensive universal forces of power; one of the few English books to proclaim a healthy scepticism about witchcraft, Reginald Scot's *A Discoverie of Witchcraft* (1584), was based on Scot's Platonist assumptions.

Popular and official or elite attitudes to magic were thus steadily drawing apart during the later sixteenth century and into the seventeenth. To be sure, there were survivals of supernatural belief across the social divide which defied Protestant hostility and scepticism: the custom of gathering to receive the royal touch against 'the King's Evil' (scrofula), for example. In one respect, supernatural preoccupations of the country's governors seemed to lead the lower orders: in the official attention to witchcraft. England participated in the mysterious paranoia about the danger of witchcraft which gripped most of Europe from the fifteenth century to the seventeenth; although Christina Larner characterised the English witchcraze as 'a faint ripple from the continental epicentre', between 500–1000 people died as a result of successive and steadily more comprehensive anti-witchcraft legislation passed by the English Parliament in 1542, 1563 and 1604.[8]

The exact impetus and the motivation for this concern is not clear; probably there is no single explanation which will account for such a widely-dispersed fear. The original initiative in all European countries seems to have been from the secular and ecclesiastical governing elites, who produced literary analyses of the supposed nature of witchcraft and then legislation to curb it. Thereafter, ordinary people reacted to official encouragement, so that in England, most prosecutions were not government-inspired, but were the result of genuine initiatives from ordinary people against their neighbours. Yet English interest in persecuting witches was patchy, and could be surprisingly localised; for instance, of 460 known prosecutions for witchcraft from Essex, 410 were from the same village. The English never showed much sign of excitement about the elaborate theories of some continental anti-witch campaigns that witches formed part of an organised devilish conspiracy against Christendom, perhaps because the requirements of English law meant that torture was rarely used to extract confessions: on the continent the use of torture was a sure way of producing confessions of whatever conspiracy theory had seized the torturer's imagination. Even after the more stringent legislation of 1604, the vast majority of prosecutions for witchcraft were concerned with specific harm done by a supposed witch (*maleficium*), rather with participation in satanic cults.[9]

The problem is to judge how much of a genuine alternative society the world of magic and witchcraft represented. We can dismiss early twentieth century fantasies about the survival of a coherent witch-cult in early modern England, but beyond this it is difficult to make any statements which can be grounded on statistics; for instance, we are indebted to Keith Thomas's great work *Religion and the Decline of Magic* for gathering a mass of evidence on magical practices, natural medicine, astrology and witchcraft, yet this treasure trove remains obstinately anecdotal. A statement based on general impressions of the written evidence is hazardous but perhaps inevitable: looking through the voluminous surviving archives of Tudor England, either official records like court proceedings or the conversation of the literate as revealed in private letters, I am impressed by how little talk there is of witches and magic. Among the articulate at least, the world of the supernatural was not a major concern. What of ordinary people? All we can say is that if they were concerned with magic rather than with official religion, their priorities left little impression on the records. Tudor governments did not generally make windows into the hearts of their subjects, and therefore rarely fully revealed the curious mixture of beliefs which might lie within the minds of humble folk – England has nothing like the tribunal archives of the medieval Spanish Inquisition which reveal such an unexpected range of scepticism and religious heterodoxy even in a late medieval society carefully regulated by the Church.[10]

One is left with the criterion which would seem least relevant to a conscientious Protestant minister of the Elizabethan Church, that of regular church attendance. How many people went to church, regardless of what they believed before they got there, and of what they believed after an hour or two of Protestant worship? Here, as in other areas of discussion, the former pessimism of historians is being modified. Notoriously the Protestant Church of England had problems particularly in many areas of the north of England, both in attracting people to church or even providing adequate accommodation for them if they wanted to come; but its pre-Reformation predecessor had experienced the same problems, and indeed had largely created them by the inadequacies of the northern parish system.

Pessimistic estimates are not borne out by the most recent investigations. Dr Ingram actually finds rising church attendance in the late sixteenth century, and the returns of communicants made on a nationwide basis in 1603 suggest at least in south-east England levels of systematic adult absence from church of no more than one or two per cent. Even in London, where it has often been asserted that population mobility and sheer numbers were a constant threat to orderly parish life, Dr Boulton's research shows a remarkable degree of efficiency where one would least expect it, in very large parishes with many poor; surviving records from the later years of Elizabeth onwards show that the authorities put a successful and sustained effort into enforcing church attendance at least at one of a carefully-organised series of Easter communion services. Just as with church courts, such efficiency and close regulation would depend on a wide measure of consent, as its rapid breakdown during the Civil Wars demonstrated. In the north of England, too, by the beginning of the seventeenth century the long-standing crisis in church accommodation, exacerbated by the loss of many chantry chapels, was being made good in a new wave of chapel-building. All this suggests a church which left little room for a world beyond, despite all the untidiness and confusion which remained a continual worry for those who wished to see England become an exemplar of the best reformed Churches.[11]

The whole story of the later English Reformation which produced the Church of England is a tale of retreat from the high-water mark of Protestant advance in 1550, when in the struggle between Hooper and his more cautious episcopal colleagues, it seemed for a moment as if the work of Reformation would progress towards the standard set by the best reformed Churches of the continent. Hooper's defeat meant that the 1552 Prayer Book represented the most radical stage which the official English Reformation would ever reach. From then on the Protestantism of the English Church was in a state of arrested development; although continental advances could sway the minds and hearts of the majority of clergy and activist laity, they could not proceed to move the structure any further forward from its idiosyncratic anchorage in the medieval past. Far from being deviants from an Anglican norm, the Elizabethan Puritans were merely trying to take up the logic of the signposts to the future represented by Hooper's stand in 1550, and force structural reform to match the theology of the people who led the Church: a symbol of this was their vain attempt to see the Edwardian attempt at a proper Protestant law-code for the church, the *Reformatio Legum*, turned into law in the 1571 Parliament. In the north of England, where the fight against conservative survival in religion was more finely-balanced than in the south, Puritans were generally taken as allies in the fight, and suffered less official harassment than in the province of Canterbury; here Elizabethan Puritanism might in many places have seemed to be achieving its aims in transforming the character of established religion.

Yet as so often in English history, it was the south and not the north which decided Puritanism's fate. The 1580s saw Puritans intimidated and thrust aside; from the 1590s, a group of churchmen began boldly to enunciate views which would take the English Church in a very different direction, and which for a brief period in the 1620s and 1630s, succeeded in capturing its leadership. The reaction of the Englishmen who had been nurtured by the Elizabethan Church was to overthrow the government which had allowed such a thing to happen; yet when a version of the 1559 Settlement was restored in 1660, never again was the established Church to prove comprehensive enough to contain the spectrum of Protestant belief which had been possible in the late sixteenth century. From this story of confusion and changing direction emerged a Church which has never subsequently dared define its identity decisively as Protestant or Catholic, and which has decided in the end that this is a virtue rather than a handicap. Perhaps the Anglican gift to the Christian story is the ability to make a virtue out of necessity.

NOTES AND REFERENCES

Summary citations are given of all works which appear in the select bibliography. Other works are cited in full once in a chapter, and are given a summary citation if mentioned again in the same chapter.

1. SETTING THE SCENE

1. Whiting, 'Reformation in the South West of England', p. 124: for discussion on London, I am grateful to Dr Susan Brigden.
2. Cf. especially Scarisbrick, *Reformation and the English People*, Chapter 2.
3. MacCulloch, *Suffolk and the Tudors*, pp. 338–9, Appendix III; Smith, *County and Court*, pp. 32, 80–6. For examples of references to government 'purges' of the commissions, cf. Jones, *Faith by Statute*, p. 23; British Library Cottonian Titus BI, fo.487v (1537), Additional MS 48023, fo.357r (1561).

2. PROTESTANT AND CATHOLIC FAILURE 1547–1558

1. Bush, *Government Policy of Protector Somerset*, and D. Hoak, *The King's Council in the reign of Edward VI* (Cambridge: Cambridge University Press, 1976) give the best accounts of the Edwardian years.
2. C. Buchanan, *What did Cranmer think he was doing?* (Nottingham: Grove Liturgical Study 7, 1976), especially p. 23.
3. Brooks, *Thomas Cranmer's Doctrine of the Eucharist*, especially p. 93.

4. J. Opie, 'The Anglicizing of John Hooper', *Archiv für Reformationsgeschichte* 59 (1968), p. 150.

5. Pettegree, *Foreign Protestant Communities*, Chapters 2–3.

6. Buchanan, *What did Cranmer think he was doing?*, pp. 21–4.

7. Cressy, *Literacy and the Social Order*, p. 166: see also C. Kitching, 'The disposal of monastic and chantry lands', in Heal and O'Day, *Church and Society in England*, Chapter 6, and Heal, *Of Prelates and Princes*, Chapter 6.

8. N. Ridley, *A Piteous Lamentation of the Miserable Estate of the Church . . .* , in *Works* (Cambridge: Parker Society, 1843), p. 59.

9. Heal, *Of Prelates and Princes*, pp. 139–40, 144–7, and cf. MacCulloch, *Suffolk and the Tudors*, p. 48. P. Hembry, 'Episcopal Palaces, 1535 to 1660', in E. W. Ives *et al.*, (eds.), *Wealth and Power in Tudor England* (London: Athlone Press, 1978).

10. MacCulloch, *Suffolk and the Tudors*, pp. 165–8, 231; Bourgeois, 'The Government of Cambridgeshire, circa 1524–88', pp. 191–3, 215; Clark, *Kent 1500–1640*, pp. 83–5, modified by J. D. Alsop, 'Latimer, the "Commonwealth of Kent" and the 1549 Rebellions', *Bulletin of Historical Research* 28 (1985), p. 381n.

11. D. MacCulloch (ed.), 'The *Vita Mariae Angliae Reginae* of Robert Wingfield of Brantham', *Camden Miscellany* 28 (Camden Soc. 4th ser. 29, 1984), pp. 191, 193; MacCulloch, *Suffolk and the Tudors*, Chapter 10.

12. Kitching, 'Disposal of monastic and chantry lands', in Heal and O'Day, *Church and Society in England*, pp. 128–36; G. Woodward, 'The dispersal of chantry lands in Somerset', *Southern History* 5 (1983), pp. 106–9.

13. Loades, *Reign of Mary Tudor*, pp. 170–7; J. Loach, *Parliament and the Crown in the Reign of Mary Tudor* (Oxford: Clarendon Press, 1986), p. 105.

14. Pogson, 'Reginald Pole and the priorities of government', pp. 18–19; J. Loach, 'Pamphlets and politics 1553–8', *Bulletin of Historical Research* 48 (1975), pp. 31–44.

15. Loach, *Parliament and the Crown in the reign of Mary Tudor*, pp. 18, 51; Pogson, 'Reginald Pole and the priorities of government', p. 12.

16. Kitch (ed.), *Studies in Sussex Church History*, p. 158; MacCulloch, *Suffolk and the Tudors*, pp. 171–3; G. Alexander, 'Bonner and the Marian persecutions', in Haigh (ed.), *English Reformation Revised*, p. 166.

17. P. Hughes, *The Reformation in England* (London: Hollis and Carter, 1954), vol. 2, pp. 231–6. R. Pogson, 'Revival and

reform in Mary Tudor's Church', in Haigh (ed.), *English Reformation Revised*, pp. 141, 150–1; R. Pogson, 'The legacy of the Schism', in Loach and Tittler (eds), *Mid-Tudor Polity*, Chapter 6.

18. Loach, *Parliament and the Crown in the reign of Mary Tudor*, especially p. 173. On JPs, see Clark, *Kent 1500–1640*, p. 98; MacCulloch, *Suffolk and the Tudors*, pp. 232–4, 338; R. Fritze, 'Faith and Faction: Religious changes, national politics and the development of local factionalism in Hampshire, 1485–1570', Cambridge Ph.D., 1982, Table III, pp. 28–9; Bourgeois, 'The Government of Cambridgeshire, circa 1524–88', pp. 62, 223.

19. J. H. Crehan, 'St Ignatius and Cardinal Pole', *Archivum Historicum Societatis Jesu* 25 (1956), pp. 72–98. On schools and universities, see Loades, *Reign of Mary Tudor*, p. 352; Dickens, *Lollards and Protestants*, p. 177; Porter, *Reformation and Reaction in Tudor Cambridge*, Chapter 4 and pp. 101–3.

20. O'Day, *English Clergy*, pp. 8, 113, 247 n. 14; R. Pogson, 'The legacy of the Schism', in Loach and Tittler (eds), *Mid-Tudor Polity*, p. 126; MacCulloch, *Suffolk and the Tudors*, p. 239.

3. 1559–1577: THE CUCKOO IN THE NEST

1. On what follows, see N. Jones, 'Elizabeth's first year: the conception and birth of the Elizabethan political world', in Haigh (ed.), *Reign of Elizabeth I*, Chapter 1; Jones, *Faith by Statute*; Hudson, *Cambridge Connection*; N. M. Sutherland, 'The Marian exiles and the establishment of the Elizabethan regime', *Archiv für Reformationsgeschichte* 78 (1987), pp. 253–86.

2. Prestwich (ed.), *International Calvinism*, p. 73.

3. Neale's thesis is best summarised in his *Elizabeth I and her Parliaments 1559–1581* (London: Jonathan Cape, 1953), pp. 33–84.

4. MacCulloch, *Suffolk and the Tudors*, pp. 182–3; R. Hutton, 'The local impact of the Tudor Reformation' in Haigh (ed.), *Reformation Revised*, p. 134.

5. W. P. Haugaard, *Elizabeth and the English Reformation* (Cambridge: Cambridge University Press, 1968), Chapter 6.

6. P. Lake, 'Matthew Hutton: a Puritan Bishop?', *History* 64 (1979), p. 189. On the 1563 Convocation, see W. P. Kennedy (ed.), *Elizabethan Episcopal Administration*, Alcuin Club Collections 25 (1924), vol. 1, p. clvii.

7. Collinson, *Elizabethan Puritan Movement*, p. 78, and for what follows, ibid., Chapters 2 and 3.
8. Knappen, *Tudor Puritanism*, p. 488.
9. Kitch (ed.), *Studies in Sussex Church History*, p. 95; MacCulloch, *Suffolk and the Tudors*, pp. 190–1.
10. MacCaffrey, *Shaping of the Elizabethan Regime*, p. 108.
11. Smith, *County and Court*, pp. 34–5; Haigh, *Reformation and Resistance*, pp. 212–13; MacCulloch, *Suffolk and the Tudors*, pp. 84–6.
12. For a detailed narrative of these years, see MacCaffrey, *Shaping of the Elizabethan Regime*; on the dating of the beginning of recusancy, see MacCulloch, *Suffolk and the Tudors*, p. 192; Haigh, *Reformation and Resistance*, p. 259, places the beginning of recusancy earlier, but gives no substantial evidence.
13. E.g. Haigh, *Reformation and Resistance*, Chapter 16; Palliser, *Tudor York*, pp. 254–5; P. Clark, 'Josias Nicholls and religious radicalism, 1553–1639', *Journal of Ecclesiastical History* 28 (1977), p. 136. For temporary conservative success in retaining influence, see Manning, *Religion and Society in Elizabethan Sussex*, Chapters 5 and 6; Smith, *County and Court*, Chapter 10; MacCulloch, *Suffolk and the Tudors*, pp. 192–3.
14. G. R. Elton, *The Parliament of England 1559–1581* (Cambridge: Cambridge University Press, 1986), pp. 205–11.
15. Ibid., pp. 214–16; Collinson, *Elizabethan Puritan Movement*, pp. 118–21.
16. The definitive (and masterly) account of these events is Collinson, *Archbishop Grindal*, Chapters 12–15.
17. Collinson, *Archbishop Grindal*, pp. 231–2.

4. POLITY AND POLICY 1577–1603

1. E. St John Brooks, *Sir Christopher Hatton* (London: Jonathan Cape, 1946), pp. 61, 210–19.
2. On the 1562–63 struggle, see MacCaffrey, *Shaping of the Elizabethan Regime*, pp. 126–37, and on Leicester's position in the 1580s, MacCaffrey, *Queen Elizabeth and the Making of Policy*, Chapters 5, 12–14, 16. Simon Adams's forthcoming biography of Leicester will further illuminate these events.
3. P. McGrath, *Papists and Puritans under Elizabeth I* (London: Blandford Press, 1967), pp. 177n, 255–6.
4. For the extent of Grindal's freedom to act as referee, see Collinson, *Archbishop Grindal*, pp. 271–2.

5. Smith, *County and Court*, Chapter 10; MacCulloch, 'Catholic and Puritan'; MacCulloch 1986, Chapter 6; Manning, *Elizabethan Sussex*, Chapters 4–6; Bourgeois, 'The Government of Cambridgeshire, circa 1524–88', Chapter 6.

6. Collinson, *Elizabethan Puritan Movement*, p. 244. The best account of the events described in the following paragraphs is ibid., pp. 243–329.

7. Collinson, *Elizabethan Puritan Movement*, pp. 218–39, and see R. G. Usher (ed.), *The Presbyterian movement in the reign of Queen Elizabeth as illustrated by the minute book of the Dedham Classis, 1582–1589* (Camden Society 3rd series 8, 1905).

8. MacCulloch, 'Catholic and Puritan', pp. 282–3; MacCulloch, *Suffolk and the Tudors*, pp. 211–12, 335, 339; Collinson, *Elizabethan Puritan Movement*, p. 278.

9. J. E. Neale, *Elizabeth I and her Parliaments 1584–1601* (London: Jonathan Cape, 1957), pp. 62–3, and on this Parliament generally, Chapters 4 and 5; on this and the following paragraph, Collinson, *Elizabethan Puritan Movement*, pp. 273–88, 291–302.

10. Collinson, *Elizabethan Puritan Movement*, pp. 304–7; MacCulloch, *Suffolk and the Tudors*, p. 216.

11. Neale, *Parliaments 1584–1601*, pp. 145–65; Collinson, *Elizabethan Puritan Movement*, pp. 306–16.

12. *The Works of John Whitgift D.D. . . . .* (Parker Soc. 1851), vol. 1, p. 184.

13. On what follows, see Lake, *Anglicans and Puritans?*, pp. 88–97.

14. L. H. Carson, *Martin Marprelate, Gentleman: Master Job Throckmorton Laid Open in his Colors* (San Marino: Huntington Library, 1981).

15. W. D. J. Cargill Thompson, 'A reconsideration of Richard Bancroft's Paul's Cross Sermon of 9 February 1588–9', *Journal of Ecclesiastical History*, 20 (1969), pp. 261–6; O. Chadwick, 'Richard Bancroft's submission', *Journal of Ecclesiastical History* 3 (1952), pp. 58–73; Neale, *Parliaments 1584–1601*, pp. 216–32; Collinson, *Elizabethan Puritan Movement*, pp. 398–400.

16. Collinson, *Elizabethan Puritan Movement*, pp. 403–31.

17. Neale, *Parliaments 1584–1601*, pp. 244–5.

18. Lake, *Anglicans and Puritans?*, pp. 196, 239–40; Tyacke, *Anti-Calvinists*, p. 203, and see below, Chapter 5.

19. Cf. e.g. Clark, *Kent 1500–1640*, pp. 249–68; MacCulloch, *Suffolk and the Tudors*, pp. 217–19, 243–52, 274–82; on the Howard recovery, see L. L. Peck, *Northampton: Patronage and Policy at the Court of James I* (London: Allen and Unwin, 1982).

20. Kendall, *Calvin and English Calvinism*, pp. 52–3.

5. THEOLOGY: CREATING A NEW ORTHODOXY

1. Parker, *The English Sabbath*.
2. For a useful discussion of early English humanism, see A. Fox and J. Guy, *Reassessing the Henrician Age. Humanism, politics and reform 1500–1550* (Oxford: Basil Blackwell, 1986), Chapter 1; also Hudson, *Cambridge Connection*.
3. J. F. Davis, 'The trials of Thomas Bilney and the English Reformation', *Historical Journal* 24 (1981), pp. 775–90.
4. C. Cross, 'Continental students and the Protestant Reformation in England in the sixteenth century', in D. Baker (ed.), *Reform and Reformation: England and the Continent c.1500–c.1750 (Studies in Church History: Subsidia 2, 1979)*, pp. 35–57; Pettegree, *Foreign Protestant Communities*, pp. 28–9.
5. John Dove, qu. Tyacke, *Anti-Calvinists*, p. 33. For a general discussion, see B. Hall, 'Early rise and gradual decline of Lutheranism in England', pp. 121–30; Christianson, 'Reformers and the Church of England', p. 469.
6. See White, 'Rise of Arminianism reconsidered'; Lake, 'Calvinism and the English Church'; debate between N. Tyacke and P. White in *Past and Present* 115 (May 1987), pp. 201–29.
7. Collinson, *Godly People*, p. 147; on Bullinger, Christianson, 'Reformers and the Church of England', pp. 470–1.
8. *The Decades of Henry Bullinger . . .* , (Parker Society, 1849), vol. 1, p. viii.
9. Dent, *Protestant Reformers*, Chapter 4, and cf. Tyacke, *Anti-Calvinists*, p. 129; Lake, *Moderate Puritans*, esp. pp. 201–3; Collinson, *Religion of Protestants*, pp. 81–3. For publication figures, see Kendall, *Calvin and English Calvinism*, pp. 52–3.
10. Ibid., pp. 28–38, and see subsequent debate between P. Helm and M. C. Bell in *Scottish Journal of Theology* 34 (1981), pp. 179–85 and 36 (1983), pp. 535–40.
11. J. Møller, 'The beginnings of Puritan covenant theology', *Journal of Ecclesiastical History* 14 (1963), pp. 62–5; cf. McGrath, *Reformation Thought*, pp. 122–4.
12. J. E. Booty, *John Jewel as apologist of the Church of England* (London: SPCK, 1963), pp. 175–6; Hall, 'The early rise and gradual decline of Lutheranism', p. 130.
13. Tyacke, *Anti-Calvinists*, p. 2; I. Green, 'The emergence of the English catechism under Elizabeth and the early Stuarts', *Journal of Ecclesiastical History* 37 (1986), pp. 406–7; W. P.

Haugaard, 'John Calvin and the catechism of Alexander Nowell', *Archiv für Reformationsgeschichte* 61 (1970), pp. 53–65.

14. Lake, *Anglicans and Puritans?*, pp. 36–8, 43. On Grindal and Bullinger, see Collinson, *Archbishop Grindal*, p. 127.

15. Porter, *Reformation and Reaction in Tudor Cambridge*, Chapter 16; Lake, *Moderate Puritans*, pp. 218–26; Tyacke, *Anti-Calvinists*, pp. 10, 31, and see the debate noted above, n. 6.

16. Tyacke, *Anti-Calvinists*, p. 249 in Appendix I, and see ibid., pp. 3, 17 on Bancroft, and on Hutton, pp. 32–3. On Bridges, Lake, 'Calvinism and the English Church', pp. 37–8; P. A. Welsby, *George Abbot: the Unwanted Archbishop 1562–1633* (London: SPCK, 1962) pp. 6, 12, 149; P. Lake, 'Matthew Hutton, a Puritan bishop?', *History* 64 (1979), p. 201.

17. Pigg: Cambridge University Library MS Dd II 75, fos. 21–5, qu. MacCulloch, *Suffolk and the Tudors*, p. 216; Travers: Lake, *Moderate Puritans*, p. 66.

18. Lake, *Moderate Puritans*, pp. 55–76, 69–71, 93–115; cf. Lake, *Anglicans and Puritans?*, p. 26. Dent, *Protestant Reformers*, pp. 147–8.

19. W. Haller, *Foxe's Book of Martyrs and the Elect Nation* (London: 1963), criticised in Firth, *Apocalyptic Tradition*, esp. pp. 107–8; cf. ibid., pp. 86, 98 on the papal Antichrist. For other criticisms of Haller, see Collinson, *Godly People*, p. 213; P. Lake, 'The significance of the Elizabethan identification of the Pope as Antichrist', *Journal of Ecclesiastical History* 31 (1980), p. 163. Cf. also Lake, *Anglicans and Puritans?*, pp. 79, 103.

20. Firth, *Apocalyptic Tradition*, pp. 136–9, 209, 215–19.

6. THEOLOGY: THE CONSENSUS CHALLENGED

1. From a letter in many versions, one pr. in *A Parte of a Register* (London 1593), pp. 128ff; for discussion, see MacCulloch, *Suffolk and the Tudors*, pp. 207–8, 343.

2. Letter in Public Record Office REQ.3/7, qu. MacCulloch, *Suffolk and the Tudors*, p. 340.

3. E. Arber (ed.), *A brief discourse of the troubles at Frankfort, 1554–1558 A.D.* (London, 1908); P. Collinson, 'The Authorship of *A Brieff Discours off the Troubles Begonne at Franckfort*', *Journal of Ecclesiastical History* 9 (1958), pp. 188–208. A good brief account is Dickens, *English Reformation*, pp. 394–400. C. Hill, *Economic Problems of the Church from Archbishop Whitgift to the Long Parliament* (Oxford: Clarendon Press, 1956).

4. Coolidge, *The Pauline Renaissance in England*, esp. Chapter 2.

5. 1 Corinthians 3.9; 2 Corinthians 6.16; 1 Peter 2.5. These and the following Biblical quotations are from the Geneva Bible of 1560.

6. Cf. the debate between Cartwright and Whitgift over this in *The Works of John Whitgift, D.D.* . . . (Parker Society, 1853), vol. 3, esp. pp. 34–5, 52–3.

7. See Lake, *Anglicans and Puritans?*, p. 32, for the debate on this between Whitgift and Cartwright.

8. Coolidge, *Pauline Renaissance in England*, pp. 58–9.

9. Kendall, *Calvin and English Calvinism*, esp. pp. 1–13, 79–80.

10. Whitgift, *Works*, vol. 1, pp. 522–4, qu. Lake, *Anglicans and Puritans?*, pp. 40–1.

11. P. Avis, 'Moses and the Magistrate: a study in the rise of Protestant legalism', *Journal of Ecclesiastical History* 26 (1975), pp. 149–72.

12. Coolidge, *Pauline Renaissance in England*, Chapter 5; Kendall, *Calvin and English Calvinism*, pp. 38–41; M. McGiffert, 'From Moses to Adam: the making of the covenant of works', *Sixteenth Century Journal* 19 (1988), pp. 132–6; but cf. cautionary remarks on connections between Heidelberg and English ideas in D. Visser, 'The Covenant in Zacharias Ursinus', *Sixteenth Century Journal* 18 (1987), pp. 532–5. On Fenner, see Knappen, *Tudor Puritanism*, pp. 373–4.

13. Coolidge, *Pauline Renaissance in England*, pp. 111–30. The quotation is from Peter Bulkeley, qu. ibid., p. 123. Cf. Knappen, *Tudor Puritanism*, p. 376.

14. W. Nijenhuis, 'Adrianus Saravia as an eirenical churchman in England and the Netherlands', in D. Baker (ed.), *Reform and Reformation: England and the Continent c.1500–c.1750 (Studies in Church History: Subsidia* 2, (1979)), pp. 153–9.

15. Tyacke, *Anti-Calvinists*, p. 36; Lake, *Anglicans and Puritans?*, p. 229.

16. Dent, *Protestant Reformers*, Chapter 5; Tyacke, *Anti-Calvinists*, Chapter 3. On Harsnet, see R. Bauckham, 'Hooker, Travers and the Church of Rome in the 1580s', *Journal of Ecclesiastical History* 29 (1978), p. 42.

17. Porter, *Reformation and Reaction*, Chapter 15, pp. 397–413; Tyacke, *Anti-Calvinists*, Chapter 2; Lake, *Moderate Puritans*, pp. 236–9; Lake, 'Calvinism and the English Church', pp. 48–9.

18. Dent, *Protestant Reformers*, p. 232; MacCulloch, *Suffolk and the Tudors*, pp. 210–11. On Montague, J. Goring, 'The Reforma-

tion of the ministry in Elizabethan Sussex', *Journal of Ecclesiastical History* 34 (1983), p. 353.

19. An excellent treatment of Hooker's thought is Lake, *Anglicans and Puritans?*, Chapter 4.

20. P. D. L. Avis, 'Richard Hooker and John Calvin', with a comment by R. Bauckham, *Journal of Ecclesiastical History* 32 (1981), pp. 29–31.

21. Lake, *Anglicans and Puritans?*, p. 145.

7. REFORMING A MINISTRY

1. P. Hughes, *The Reformation in England* (London, Hollis and Carter, 1954). vol. 1, pp. 31–2.

2. Collinson, *Godly People*, pp. 169–71; Collinson, *Religion of Protestants*, pp. 23–4.

3. R. A. Houlbrooke (ed.), *The Letter Book of John Parkhurst* (Norfolk Record Society 43, 1975), introduction, *passim*; R. O'Day, 'Thomas Bentham: a case study in the problems of the early Elizabethan episcopate', *Journal of Ecclesiastical History* 23 (1972), pp. 137–59; Heal, *Of Prelates and Princes*, p. 260.

4. O'Day, 'Thomas Bentham', pp. 152–3; O'Day, *English Clergy*, p. 43; Houlbrooke, *Church Courts and the People*, p. 34; on Becon's scheme see *Calendar of the Manuscripts . . . At Hatfield House . . .* (Historical MSS Commission, 1888) vol. 2, pp. 195–8, and cf. Smith, *County and Court*, p. 210–12. On peculiars, R. Peters, *Oculus Episcopi. Administration in the Archdeaconry of St. Albans 1580–1625* (Manchester: Manchester University Press, 1966), p. 2; H. G. Owen, 'A nursery of Elizabethan nonconformity, 1567–72', *Journal of Ecclesiastical History* 11 (1966), pp. 217–22; O'Day, *English Clergy*, p. 34.

5. Collinson, *Religion of Protestants*, p. 60; Heal, *Of Prelates and Princes*.

6. Houlbrooke (ed.), *Letter Book of John Parkhurst*, p. 171.

7. Collinson, *Religion of Protestants*, pp. 49–52.

8. D. M. Owen, 'Synods in the Diocese of Ely in the later Middle Ages and the sixteenth century', in G. Cuming (ed.), *Studies in Church History* vol. 3 (1966), pp. 217–22; Peters, *Oculus Episcopi*, pp. 45–50; Collinson, *Religion of Protestants*, pp. 66–8, 112, 122–9; H. G. Owen, 'The episcopal visitation: its limits and limitations in Elizabethan London', *Journal of Ecclesiastical History* 11 (1960), pp. 179–85.

9. Cf. e.g. Houlbrooke, *Church Courts and the People*, pp. 24–5; Ingram, *Church Courts, Sex and Marriage*, p. 64; D. MacCul-

loch, 'Bondmen under the Tudors' in C. Cross *et al.*, (eds.), *Law and Government under the Tudors* (Cambridge: Cambridge University Press, 1988), p. 107.

10. Cf. especially F. D. Price, 'The abuses of excommunication and the decline of ecclesiastical discipline under Queen Elizabeth', *English Historical Review* 57 (1942), pp. 106–15.

11. Ingram, *Church Courts, Sex and Marriage*, Chapter 1, is a particularly useful bibliographical discussion. On suspension and excommunication, see ibid., p. 53 and Houlbrooke, *Church Courts and the People*, pp. 48–9.

12. Manning, 'Crisis of episcopal authority', pp. 3, 14.

13. Collinson, *Religion of Protestants*, p. 56; P. Tyler, 'The significance of the ecclesiastical commission at York', *Northern History* 2 (1967), pp. 27–44.

14. J. S. Purvis, 'The registers of Archbishops Lee and Holgate', *Journal of Ecclesiastical History* 13 (1962), p. 190; F. Heal, 'The parish clergy and the Reformation in the diocese of Ely', *Proceedings of the Cambridge Antiquarian Society* 66 (1977), p. 154; G. A. J. Hodgett, 'The unpensioned ex-religious in Tudor England', *Journal of Ecclesiastical History* 13 (1962), p. 201.

15. Bowker, 'The Henrician Reformation and the parish clergy', in Haigh (ed.), *English Reformation Revised*, Chapter 4. On clerical career structure, see Zell, 'Personnel of the clergy in Kent', and for suggested modifications to Zell's picture on clerical incomes, J. Pound, 'Clerical poverty in early sixteenth century England: some East Anglian evidence', *Journal of Ecclesiastical History* 37 (1986), pp. 389–96.

16. T. J. McCann, 'The clergy and the Elizabethan Settlement in the diocese of Chichester', in Kitch (ed.), *Studies in Sussex Church History*, pp. 110–11; for a much lower East Anglian figure, see MacCulloch, *Suffolk and the Tudors*, p. 182.

17. O'Day, *English Clergy*, p. 130; Collinson, *Godly People*, p. 38.

18. J. I. Daeley, 'Pluralism in the diocese of Canterbury ... 1559–1575', *Journal of Ecclesiastical History* 18 (1967), especially p. 47.

19. On this and following paragraphs, see O'Day, *English Clergy*, Chapter 4 and pp. 69–72; Collinson, *Religion of Protestants*, pp. 94–5; O'Day, *Education and Society*, p. 103 and Chapter 7.

20. Hinderclay: MacCulloch, *Suffolk and the Tudors*, p. 319. Overton: O'Day, *English Clergy*, pp. 68–9.

21. Collinson, *Religion of Protestants*, pp. 172–7.

22. Collinson, *Godly People*, pp. 469–513; cf. particularly his

remarks on the 'alienated intellectual' thesis of Mark Curtis, ibid. p. 469.
23. Ibid., p. 301.
24. C. Cross, '"Dens of loitering lubbers": Protestant protest against cathedral foundations, 1540–1640', in D. Baker (ed.), *Schism, heresy and religious protest* (*Studies in Church History* 9, 1972), pp. 231–8; L. M. Hill, *Bench and Bureaucracy. The public career of Sir Julius Caesar 1580–1636* (Stanford: Stanford University Press, 1988), pp. 62–3.
25. S. E. Lehmberg, 'The reformation of choirs: cathedral musical establishments in Tudor England', in D. J. Guth and J. W. McKenna, *Tudor Rule and Revolution* (Cambridge: Cambridge University Press, 1982), pp. 45–68; N. Temperley, *The Music of the English Parish Church* (2 vols. Cambridge University Press, 1980).

8.   THE RECEPTION OF THE REFORMATION

1. A useful bibliographical discussion is Haigh, *English Reformation Revised*, Chapter 1.
2. Dickens, 'Early expansion of Protestantism', pp. 200–11.
3. On Whalley, see C. Haigh, 'Puritan evangelism in the reign of Elizabeth I', *English Historical Review* 92 (1977), p. 39; cf. Richardson, *Puritanism in north-west England*, pp. 15–17.
4. MacCulloch, *Suffolk and the Tudors*, p. 142; C. Burgess, '"By Quick and by dead: wills and pious provision in late medieval Bristol', *English Historical Review* 102 (1987), p. 857; C. Phythian-Adams, *Desolation of a City: Coventry and the urban crisis of the late Middle Ages* (Cambridge: Cambridge University Press, 1979), p. 287.
5. A. Kreider, *English Chantries: the road to dissolution* (Cambridge, Mass.: Harvard University Press, 1979), pp. 90–1; J. T. Rosenthal, 'The Yorkshire Chantry certificates of 1546: an analysis', *Northern History* 9 (1974), p. 30. On the Pilgrimage, see Haigh, *Reformation and Resistance*, Chapter 9, and for a similar emphasis on the role of the monasteries in the Cumbrian part of the Pilgrimage, the forthcoming work of my Ph.D. student Margaret Clark.
6. One of the most detailed studies of the use of wills alongside other documents is Spufford, *Contrasting Communities*, Chapter 13.
7. R. Hutton, 'The local impact of the Tudor Reformations' in Haigh (ed.) *English Reformation Revised*, p. 118; Whiting,

'Reformation in the South West', pp. 40, 49, 56, 172–6, and Whiting, 'Prayers for the dead'. For summary discussion on wills, see Dickens, 'Early expansion of Protestantism', pp. 214–17.

8. Palliser, *Tudor York*, pp. 250–1; Dickens, *Lollards and Protestants*, pp. 171–2; Mayhew, 'Reformation in east Sussex'; Bowker, *The Henrician Reformation: the diocese of Lincoln under John Longland 1521–1547* (Cambridge University Press, 1981), pp. 176–8.

9. A. G. Dickens (ed.), 'Robert Parkyn's narrative of the Reformation', *English Historical Review* 62 (1947), pp. 68–73; on Cumbria, communication from Mrs Margaret Clark; MacCulloch, *Suffolk and the Tudors*, pp. 169–70.

10. Clark, *Kent 1500–1640*, pp. 75–6; Peet, 'Mid-sixteenth century parish clergy', p. 223; Palliser, *Tudor York*, pp. 250–1; Whiting, 'Prayers for the dead', pp. 79, 87; cf. discussion by D. M. Palliser in Heal and O'Day (eds.), *Church and Society in England*, pp. 39–40.

11. J. Youings, 'The South-Western Rebellion of 1549', *Southern History* 1 (1979), pp. 99–122; D. MacCulloch, 'Kett's Rebellion in Context', in P. Slack (ed.), *Rebellion, Popular Protest and the Social Order in Early Modern England* (Cambridge: Cambridge University Press, 1984), pp. 39–76; Clark, *Kent 1500–1640*, pp. 78–80.

12. Dickens, *Lollards and Protestants*, p. 221; Mayhew, 'Reformation in east Sussex', p. 46.

13. Hutton, 'Local impact of the Tudor Reformations', p. 131; Whiting, 'Prayers for the dead', pp. 82–3; Loades, *Reign of Mary Tudor*, pp. 352–5.

14. Kitch (ed.), *Studies in Sussex Church History*, pp. 94–6; C. H. Garrett, *The Marian exiles: a study in the origins of Elizabethan Puritanism* (Cambridge: Cambridge University Press, 1938).

15. Dickens, *Lollards and Protestants*, pp. 220–1; Peet, 'Mid-sixteenth century parish clergy', p. 223; Mayhew, 'Reformation in east Sussex', pp. 46–7. On Parkyn, A. G. Dickens, 'The last medieval Englishman', in P. Newman Brooks (ed.), *Christian Spirituality: Essays in honour of Gordon Rupp* (London: SCM Press, 1975), p. 163.

16. W. P. Kennedy (ed.), *Elizabethan Episcopal Administration* (Alcuin Club Collections 25, 1924), vol. 1, p. xliii; R. O'Day, 'Thomas Bentham: a case study in the problems of the early Elizabethan episcopate', *Journal of Ecclesiastical History* 23 (1972), p. 145.

17. Cf. Palliser, *Tudor York*, p. 247.
18. T. J. McCann, 'The clergy and the Elizabethan Settlement in the diocese of Chichester', in Kitch (ed.), *Studies in Sussex Church History*, pp. 100–1; Hutton, 'Local impact of the Tudor Reformations', p. 135.
19. Haigh, *Reformation and Resistance*, pp. 219–20; R. B. Manning, 'The making of a protestant aristocracy: the ecclesiastical commission of the diocese of Chester, 1550–98', *Bulletin of the Institute of Historical Research*, p. 64; Hilton, 'The Cumbrian Catholics'; Hilton, 'Catholicism in Elizabethan Northumberland', p. 53; P. Tyler, 'The church courts at York and witchcraft prosecutions 1567–1640', *Northern History* 2 (1969), pp. 102–4.
20. P. R. Roberts, 'The union with England and the identity of "Anglican" Wales', *Transactions of the Royal Historical Society* 5th series 22 (1972), pp. 49–70; Williams, *Recovery, Reorientation and Reformation*, pp. 297–8.
21. A. Woodger, 'Post-Reformation mixed Gothic in Huntingdonshire churches and its campanological associations', *Archaeological Journal* 141 (1984), pp. 296–308, and cf. MacCulloch, *Suffolk and the Tudors*, pp. 346–7. For continued Catholic interest in church building, see below, Chapter 9. On communion attendance, see Boulton, 'Limits of formal religion', pp. 138–42.
22. C. Haigh (ed.), *English Reformation Revised*, Chapter 3, repr. from *History* 68 (1983), and cf. Haigh, 'Puritan Evangelism in the reign of Elizabeth I'. For a notable riposte, see Dickens, 'The shape of anticlericalism and the English Reformation'.
23. Ingram, *Church Courts, Sex and Marriage*, pp. 344–5, 350, 353–5.
24. Ibid., pp. 174, 192–209, 218–21, 230–4, 371.

9. PRINCIPLED DISSENT

1. Haigh, *Reformation and Resistance*, pp. 330–1; Richardson, *Puritanism in north-west England*, pp. 161–7.
2. A good account of the problems is A. Pritchard, *Catholic Loyalism in Elizabethan England* (London: Scolar Press, 1979), Chapters 4–10.
3. Bossy, *English Catholic Community*, p. 397.
4. See especially Haigh (ed.), *English Reformation Revised*, Chapter 9, repr. from *Past and Present* 93, with agreement from A. D. Wright, 'Catholic history, North and South', *Northern*

History 14 (1978), pp. 126–51. C. Haigh, 'From monopoly to minority: Catholicism in early modern England', *Transactions of the Royal Historical Society* 31 (1981), and Haigh, 'Revisionism, the Reformation and the history of English Catholicism', with a comment from P. McGrath, ibid.

5. MacCulloch, *Suffolk and the Tudors*, pp. 187–9, 234–5; Hilton, 'Catholicism in Elizabethan Northumberland', pp. 44–45.
6. Cf. D. Dymond and E. Martin (eds.), *An Historical Atlas of Suffolk* (Suffolk County Council, 1988), pp. 58–9, and discussion in MacCulloch, *Suffolk and the Tudors*, pp. 38–40, Chapters 4–6, pp. 320–1.
7. J. Bossy, 'The character of Elizabethan Catholicism', *Past and Present* 21 (April 1962), p. 57.
8. Cf. J. C. H. Aveling, 'Catholic households in Yorkshire, 1580–1603', *Northern History* 16 (1980), pp. 86–7, 101; Hilton, 'Catholicism in Elizabethan Northumberland', p. 57.
9. E.g. MacCulloch, *Suffolk and the Tudors*, pp. 251–3.
10. F. X. Walker, 'The implementation of the Elizabethan statutes against recusants 1581–1603', University of London Ph.D., 1961; MacCulloch, 'Catholic and Puritan', pp. 257–61.
11. P. Holmes, 'The authorship of "Leicester's Commonwealth"', *Journal of Ecclesiastical History* 33 (1982), pp. 426–7.
12. MacCulloch, *Suffolk and the Tudors*, pp. 181–82.
13. D. M. Loades, 'Anabaptism and English sectarianism in the mid-sixteenth century', in D. Baker (ed.), *Reform and Reformation: England and the Continent c.1550–c.1750 (Studies in Church History: Subsidia 2*, 1979), p. 63.
14. D. Plumb, 'The social and economic spread of rural Lollardy: a reappraisal', in W. J. Sheils and D. Wood (eds), *Voluntary Religion (Studies in Church History* 23, 1986); A. Hope, 'Lollardy: the stone the builders rejected?', in P. Lake and M. Dowling (eds), *Protestantism and the National Church in sixteenth century England* (London: Croom Helm, 1988).
15. F. Heal, 'The Family of Love and the diocese of Ely', in D. Baker (ed.), *Schism, Heresy and Religious Protest (Studies in Church History* 9, 1972), pp. 213–22; A. Hamilton, *The Family of Love* (Cambridge: Cambridge University Press, 1981); Martin, 'Elizabethan Familists'; Marsh, 'Family of Love in the parish of Balsham'. On polemic against Rome and radicals, see above, Chapter 5.
16. Martin, 'The first that made separation', and see Marsh, 'Family of Love in the parish of Balsham', p. 197n.
17. Loades, 'Anabaptism and English sectarianism', pp. 66–7; J.

W. Martin, 'The Protestant underground congregations of Mary's reign', *Journal of Ecclesiastical History* 35 (1984), pp. 519–38; Davis, *Heresy and Reformation in the south-east of England*, pp. 146–7.

18. Collinson, *Elizabethan Puritan Movement*, pp. 84–91; White, *English Separatist Tradition*, pp. 28–9; M. E. Moody, 'Trials and travels of a Nonconformist layman: the spiritual odyssey of Stephen Offwood, 1564–c.1635', *Church History* 51 (1982), p. 159.

19. Collinson, *Godly People*, p. 16; Moody, 'The spiritual odyssey of Stephen Offwood', p. 159; Collinson, 'The English Conventicle', pp. 240–1. On the lack of northern separatism, Richardson, *Puritanism in north-west England*, p. 86.

20. Collinson, *Religion of Protestants*, pp. 268–73; Collinson, 'The English Conventicle', pp. 253–9; N. Tyacke, 'Popular Puritan mentality in late Elizabethan England', in P. Clark *et al.* (eds), *The English Commonwealth 1547–1640* (New York: Barnes and Noble, 1979). Cf. Boulton, 'Limits of formal religion', pp. 135–41.

21. The best account of this and the following is White, *English Separatist Tradition*.

22. On the executions of the 1580s, see MacCulloch, *Suffolk and the Tudors*, pp. 206–8.

23. White, 'English Separatists and John Smyth revisited'; Brachlow, 'Puritan theology and General Baptist origins', and for arguments for Anabaptist influence, Coggins, 'Theological positions of John Smyth'.

24. Brachlow, 'Elizabethan roots of Henry Jacob's churchmanship'.

10.   CONCLUSION: A WORLD BEYOND?

1. Cf. e.g. J. Delumeau, *Catholicism between Luther and Voltaire: a new view of the Counter-Reformation* (London: Burns and Oates, 1977).

2. Collinson, *Religion of Protestants*, Chapter 5.

3. Cressy, *Literacy and the Social Order*, pp. 62–103, 145–7, 156–7.

4. Collinson, *Godly People*, p. 4; Wrightson and Levine, *Terling 1525–1700*; Clark, *English Alehouse*.

5. M. Spufford, 'Can we count the "Godly" and "Conformable" in the seventeenth century?', *Journal of Ecclesiastical History* 36 (1985), esp. pp. 435–6; Collinson, *Religion of Protestants*, pp.

219–20; Ingram, *Church Courts, Sex and Marriage*, pp. 353–5; Clark, *English alehouse*, p. 147.

6. Ibid., p. 159.
7. I. Green, 'The emergence of the English catechism under Elizabeth and the early Stuarts', *Journal of Ecclesiastical History* 37 (1986), pp. 397–425. We look forward to the publication of Dr Tessa Watt's research on the Elizabethan use of devotional pictures by Cambridge University Press.
8. Larner, *Witchcraft and Religion*, p. 52.
9. Macfarlane, *Witchcraft in Tudor and Stuart England*; Levack, *Witch-hunt in early modern Europe*, pp. 182–7.
10. J. Edwards, 'Religious faith and doubt in late medieval Spain: Soria *circa* 1450–1500', *Past and Present* 120 (August 1988), pp. 3–25.
11. Marchant, *Church under the Law*, pp. 218–20; Clark, *Kent 1500–1640*, p. 156; Ingram, *Church Courts, Sex and Marriage*, p. 108; Boulton, 'Limits of formal religion', and for a post-Reformation comparison, D. Spaeth in Wright, *Parish, Church and People*, pp. 125–51. On northern chapel-building see e.g. Cliffe, *Yorkshire Gentry*, pp. 262ff.

SELECT BIBLIOGRAPHY

This is a very selective guide to secondary sources, first books, then articles, then unpublished dissertations, particularly those which illustrate recent debates and developments in scholarship. Those which contain particularly useful bibliographies are marked*.

BOOKS

*G. W. O. Addleshaw and F. Etchells, *The architectural setting of Anglican Worship* (London: Faber & Faber, 1948).

M. Aston, *England's Iconoclasts: 1. Laws against Images* (Oxford: Clarendon Press, 1988).

*J. H. Aveling, *The Handle and the Axe: the Catholic Recusants in England from Reformation to Emancipation* (London: Blond & Briggs, 1976).

J. Bossy, *The English Catholic Community 1570–1850* (London: Darton, Longman & Todd, 1975).

P. N. Brooks, *Thomas Cranmer's Doctrine of the Eucharist* (London: Macmillan, 1965).

M. L. Bush, *The Government Policy of Protector Somerset* (London: Edward Arnold, 1977).

P. Clark, *English Provincial Society from the Reformation to the Revolution: . . . . Kent 1500–1640* (Hassocks: Harvester, 1977).

P. Clark, *The English Alehouse: a social history* (London: Longman, 1983).

J. T. Cliffe, *The Yorkshire Gentry, from the Reformation to the Civil War* (London: Athlone Press, 1969).

P. Collinson, *The Elizabethan Puritan Movement* (London: Jonathan Cape, 1967).

P. Collinson, *Archbishop Grindal, 1519–1583* (London: Jonathan Cape, 1979).

P. Collinson, *The Religion of Protestants* (Oxford: Clarendon Press, 1983).

P. Collinson, *Godly People, Essays on English Protestantism and Puritanism* (London: Hambledon Press, 1983).

*J. S. Coolidge, *The Pauline Renaissance in England* (Oxford: Clarendon Press, 1970).

D. Cressy, *Literacy and the Social Order* (Cambridge University Press, 1980).

*C. Cross, *Church and People 1450–1660* (London: Fontana/ Brighton: Harvester, 1976).

*C. S. L. Davies, *Peace, Print and Protestantism 1450–1558* (St Albans: Paladin, 1977).

J. F. Davis, *Heresy and Reformation in the South East of England, 1520–1559* (London: Royal Historical Society Studies in History 34, 1983).

C. M. Dent, *Protestant Reformers in Elizabethan Oxford* (Oxford: Clarendon Press, 1983).

*A. G. Dickens, *The English Reformation* (London: Fontana, 1964).

A. G. Dickens, *Lollards and Protestants in the Diocese of York 1509–1558* (New edn. London: Hambledon, 1982).

*G. R. Elton, *Reform and Reformation 1509–1558* (London: Edward Arnold, 1977).

*G. R. Elton, *The Tudor Constitution* (revised edn. Cambridge University Press, 1986).

*K. R. Firth, *The Apocalyptic Tradition in Reformation Britain 1530–1645* (Oxford: Clarendon Press, 1979).

*J. Guy, *Tudor England* (Oxford: Clarendon Press, 1988).

C. Haigh, *Reformation and Resistance in Tudor Lancashire* (Cambridge University Press, 1976).

*C. Haigh (ed.), *The Reign of Elizabeth I* (Basingstoke: Macmillan, 1984).

C. Haigh (ed.), *The English Reformation Revised* (Cambridge University Press, 1987).

F. Heal, *Of Prelates and Princes. A Study of the Economic and social Position of the Tudor Episcopate* (Cambridge University Press, 1980).

*F. Heal and R. O'Day (eds), *Church and Society in England: Henry VIII to James I* (Basingstoke: Macmillan, 1977).

I. B. Horst, *The Radical Brethren. Anabaptism and the English Reformation to 1558* (Nieuwkoop: B. de Graaf, 1972).

*R. Houlbrooke, *Church Courts and the People during the English*

Reformation 1520–70 (Oxford: Clarendon Press, 1979).

W. H. Hudson, *The Cambridge Connection and the Elizabethan Settlement of 1559* (Durham, N.C.: Duke University Press, 1980).

*M. Ingram, *Church Courts, Sex and Marriage in England, 1570–1642* (Cambridge University Press, 1987).

N. Jones, *Faith by Statute: Parliament and the Settlement of Religion, 1559* (London: Royal Historical Society Studies in History 32, 1982).

H. Kearney, *Scholars and Gentlemen. Universities and Society in Pre-Industrial Britain* (London: Faber & Faber, 1970).

*R. T. Kendall, *Calvin and English Calvinism to 1649* (Oxford: Clarendon Press, 1979).

M. J. Kitch (ed.), *Studies in Sussex Church History* (Brighton: University of Sussex Press, 1981).

M. M. Knappen, *Tudor Puritanism. A Chapter in the History of Idealism* (New edn., Chicago University Press, 1970).

P. Lake, *Moderate Puritans and the Elizabethan Church* (Cambridge University Press, 1983)

*P. Lake, *Anglicans and Puritans? Presbyterianism and English Conformist Thought from Whitgift to Hooker* (London: Unwin Hyman, 1988).

C. Larner, *Witchcraft and Religion. The politics of popular belief* (Oxford: Basil Blackwell, 1984).

*B. P. Levack, *The Witch-hunt in Early Modern Europe* (London: Longmans, 1987).

J. Loach and R. Tittler (eds.), *The mid-Tudor Polity, c. 1540–1560* (Basingstoke: Macmillan, 1980).

D. M. Loades, *The Oxford Martyrs* (London: Batsford, 1970).

*D. M. Loades, *The Reign of Mary Tudor* (London: Ernest Benn, 1979).

W. MacCaffrey, *The Shaping of the Elizabethan Regime* (Princeton University Press, 1968)

W. MacCaffrey, *Queen Elizabeth and the Making of Policy* (Princeton University Press, 1980).

D. MacCulloch, *Suffolk and the Tudors* (Oxford: Clarendon Press, 1986).

A. Macfarlane, *Witchcraft in Tudor and Stuart England* (London: Routledge, 1970).

R. B. Manning, *Religion and Society in Elizabethan Sussex* (Leicester University Press, 1969).

R. A. Marchant, *The Puritans and the Church Courts in the Diocese of York 1560–1642* (Cambridge University Press, 1960).

R. A. Marchant, *The Church under the Law: Justice, Administration and*

Discipline in the Diocese of York 1560–1640 (Cambridge University Press, 1969).

*J. Morgan, *Godly Learning: Puritan Attitudes to Reason, Learning and Education* (Cambridge University Press, 1986).

R. O'Day, *The English Clergy. The Emergence and Consolidation of a Profession 1558–1642* (Leicester University Press, 1979).

*R. O'Day, *Education and Society 1500–1800* (London: Longman, 1982).

R. O'Day and F. Heal (eds), *Continuity and Change. Personnel and Administration of the Church in England 1500–1642* (Leicester University Press, 1976).

D. M. Palliser, *Tudor York* (Oxford: Clarendon Press, 1979).

*D. M. Palliser, *The Age of Elizabeth: England under the later Tudors 1547–1603* (London: Longman, 1983).

K. L. Parker, *The English Sabbath: a study of doctrine and discipline from the reformation to the civil war* (Cambridge University Press, 1987).

A. Pettegree, *Foreign Protestant Communities in Sixteenth Century London* (Oxford: Clarendon Press, 1986).

H. C. Porter, *Reformation and Reaction in Tudor Cambridge* (New edn., Shoe String/Clio, 1983).

*M. Prestwich (ed.), *International Calvinism 1558–1715* (Oxford: Clarendon Press, 1985).

R. C. Richardson, *Puritanism in north-west England* (Manchester University Press, 1972).

E. Rose, *Cases of Conscience: Alternatives open to Recusants and Puritans under Elizabeth I and James I* (Cambridge University Press, 1975).

J. J. Scarisbrick, *The Reformation and the English People* (Oxford: Clarendon Press, 1982).

A. H. Smith, *County and Court. Government and Politics in Norfolk 1558–1603* (Oxford: Clarendon Press, 1974).

M. Spufford, *Contrasting Communities. English Villagers in the Sixteenth and Seventeenth Centuries* (Oxford: Clarendon Press, 1974).

*K. Thomas, *Religion and the Decline of Magic* (London: Weidenfeld & Nicolson, 1971).

*N. Tyacke, *Anti-Calvinists. The rise of English Arminianism c.1590–1640* (Oxford: Clarendon Press, 1987).

M. Watts, *The Dissenters. Vol. 1: from the Reformation to the French Revolution* (Oxford: Clarendon Press, 1979).

*B. R. White, *The English Separatist Tradition* (Oxford: Clarendon Press, 1971).

R. Whiting, *The Blind Devotion of the People: popular religion and the English Reformation* (Cambridge University Press, 1989).

Select Bibliography

G. Williams, *Welsh Reformation Essays* (Cardiff: University of Wales Press, 1967).

*G. Williams, *Recovery, Reorientation and Reformation in Wales c.1415–1642* (Oxford: Clarendon Press, 1987).

S. Wright (ed.), *Parish, Church and People: local studies in lay religion 1350–1750* (London: Hutchinson, 1988).

*K. Wrightson, *English Society 1580–1660* (London: Hutchinson, 1982).

K. Wrightson and D. Levine, *Poverty and Piety in an English Village: Terling 1525–1700* (New York: Academic Press, 1979).

ARTICLES

J. P. Boulton, 'The Limits of Formal Religion: the administration of Holy Communion in late Elizabethan and early Stuart London', *London Journal* 10 (1984), pp. 135–54.

S. Brachlow, 'Puritan Theology and General Baptist origins', *Baptist Quarterly* 31 (1985), pp. 179–93: *response to Coggins article below.*

S. Brachlow, 'The Elizabethan Roots of Henry Jacob's Churchmanship', *Journal of Ecclesiastical History* 36 (1985), pp. 228–54.

S. Brigden, 'Youth and the English Reformation', *Past and Present* 95 (May 1982), pp. 37–67.

P. Christianson, 'Reformers and the Church of England Under Elizabeth I and the early Stuarts', with a comment by P. Collinson, *Journal of Ecclesiastical History* 31 (1980), pp. 463–88.

J. R. Coggins, 'The Theological Positions of John Smyth', *Baptist Quarterly* 30 (1984), pp. 247–64.

P. Collinson, 'The English Conventicle', in W. J. Shiels and D. Wood (eds), *Voluntary Religion* (*Studies in Church History* 23 (1986)).

A. G. Dickens, 'The Early Expansion of Protestantism in England 1520–1558', *Archiv für Reformationsgeschichte* 78 (1987), pp. 187–222.

A. G. Dickens, 'The Shape of Anticlericalism and the English Reformation', in E. I. Kouri and T. Scott (eds.), *Politics and Society in Reformation Europe* (Basingstoke: Macmillan, 1987), pp. 379–410.

G. R. Elton, 'England and the Continent in the Sixteenth Century', in Elton, *Studies in Tudor and Stuart Politics and Government* vol. 3 (Cambridge: Cambridge University Press, 1983), pp. 305–20.

193

C. Haigh, 'Revisionism, the Reformation and the History of English Catholicism', with a Comment by P. McGrath, *Journal of Ecclesiastical History* 36 (1985), pp. 394–406.

B. Hall, 'The Early Rise and Gradual decline of Lutheranism in England (1520–1660)', in D. Baker (ed.), *Reform and Reformation: England and the Continent c.1500–c.1750* (1979), pp. 103–31.

J. A. Hilton, 'Catholicism in Elizabethan Northumberland', *Northern History* 13 (1977), pp. 44–58.

J. A. Hilton, 'The Cumbrian Catholics', *Northern History* 16 (1980), pp. 40–58.

P. Lake, 'Puritan identities', *Journal of Ecclesiastical History* 35 (1984), pp. 112–23.

P. Lake, 'Calvinism and the English Church 1570–1635', *Past and Present* 114 (Feb. 1987), pp. 32–76.

D. MacCulloch, 'Catholic and Puritan in Elizabethan Suffolk: a county community polarises', in *Archiv für Reformationsgeschichte* 72 (1981), pp. 232–89.

P. McGrath, 'Elizabethan Catholicism: a Reconsideration', *Journal of Ecclesiastical History* 35 (1984), pp. 414–28.

*J. C. McLelland, 'Calvinism perfecting Thomism? Peter Martyr Vermigli's Question', *Scottish Journal of Theology* 31 (1978), pp. 571–8.

R. B. Manning, 'The Crisis of Episcopal Authority during the Reign of Elizabeth I', *Journal of British Studies* 11 (November 1971), pp. 1–25.

C. Marsh, '"A Graceless and Audacious Companie": The Family of Love in the Parish of Balsham, 1550–1630', in W. J. Sheils and D. Wood (eds), *Voluntary Religion* (*Studies in Church History* 23 (1986)), pp. 191–208.

J. W. Martin, 'The First that made Separation from the Reformed Church of England', *Archiv für Reformationsgeschichte* 77 (1986), pp. 281–312.

J. W. Martin, 'The Elizabethan Familists', *Baptist Quarterly*, 29 (1982), pp. 267–81.

G. J. Mayhew, 'The Progress of the Reformation in East Sussex 1530–1559: the evidence from wills', *Southern History* 5 (1983), pp. 38–67.

J. Møller, 'The Beginnings of Puritan Covenant Theology', *Journal of Ecclesiastical History* 14 (1963), pp. 46–67.

R. G. Pogson, 'Reginald Pole and the Priorities of Government in Mary Tudor's Church', *Historical Journal* 18 (1975), pp. 3–20.

K. G. Powell, 'The Social Background to the Reformation in Gloucestershire', *Transactions of the Bristol and Gloucestershire*

Archaeological Society (1971), pp. 141–57.
B. R. White, 'The English Separatists and John Smyth revisited', *Baptist Quarterly* 30 (1984), pp. 344–7: *response to Coggins article above.*
P. White, 'The Rise of Arminianism Reconsidered', *Past and Present* 101 (November 1983), pp. 34–54.
R. Whiting, 'Prayers for the Dead in the Tudor South-West', *Southern History* 5 (1983), pp. 66–94.
M. Zell, 'The Personnel of the Clergy in Kent, in the Reformation Period', *English Historical Review* 89 (1974), pp. 513–33.
M. Zell, 'The Use of Religious Preambles as a Measure of Religious Belief in the Sixteenth Century', *Bulletin of the Institute of Historical Research* 50 (1977), pp. 246–9.

DISSERTATIONS

E. J. Bourgeois II, 'A Ruling Elite: the Government of Cambridgeshire, circa 1524–88', Cambridge University Ph.D., 1988.
D. J. Peet, 'The Mid-Sixteenth Century Parish Clergy, with particular consideration of the dioceses of Norwich and York', Cambridge University Ph.D., 1980.
R. Whiting, 'The Reformation in the South West of England', Exeter University Ph.D., 1977.

INDEX

G. Williams, *Welsh Reformation Essays* (Cardiff: University of Wales Press, 1967).

*G. Williams, *Recovery, Reorientation and Reformation in Wales c.1415–1642* (Oxford: Clarendon Press, 1987).

S. Wright (ed.), *Parish, Church and People: local studies in lay religion 1350–1750* (London: Hutchinson, 1988).

*K. Wrightson, *English Society 1580–1660* (London: Hutchinson, 1982).

K. Wrightson and D. Levine, *Poverty and Piety in an English Village: Terling 1525–1700* (New York: Academic Press, 1979).

ARTICLES

J. P. Boulton, 'The Limits of Formal Religion: the administration of Holy Communion in late Elizabethan and early Stuart London', *London Journal* 10 (1984), pp. 135–54.

S. Brachlow, 'Puritan Theology and General Baptist origins', *Baptist Quarterly* 31 (1985), pp. 179–93: *response to Coggins article below.*

S. Brachlow, 'The Elizabethan Roots of Henry Jacob's Churchmanship', *Journal of Ecclesiastical History* 36 (1985), pp. 228–54.

S. Brigden, 'Youth and the English Reformation', *Past and Present* 95 (May 1982), pp. 37–67.

P. Christianson, 'Reformers and the Church of England Under Elizabeth I and the early Stuarts', with a comment by P. Collinson, *Journal of Ecclesiastical History* 31 (1980), pp. 463–88.

J. R. Coggins, 'The Theological Positions of John Smyth', *Baptist Quarterly* 30 (1984), pp. 247–64.

P. Collinson, 'The English Conventicle', in W. J. Shiels and D. Wood (eds), *Voluntary Religion* (Studies in Church History 23 (1986)).

A. G. Dickens, 'The Early Expansion of Protestantism in England 1520–1558', *Archiv für Reformationsgeschichte* 78 (1987), pp. 187–222.

A. G. Dickens, 'The Shape of Anticlericalism and the English Reformation', in E. I. Kouri and T. Scott (eds.), *Politics and Society in Reformation Europe* (Basingstoke: Macmillan, 1987), pp. 379–410.

G. R. Elton, 'England and the Continent in the Sixteenth Century', in Elton, *Studies in Tudor and Stuart Politics and Government* vol. 3 (Cambridge: Cambridge University Press, 1983), pp. 305–20.

C. Haigh, 'Revisionism, the Reformation and the History of English Catholicism', with a Comment by P. McGrath, *Journal of Ecclesiastical History* 36 (1985), pp. 394–406.

B. Hall, 'The Early Rise and Gradual decline of Lutheranism in England (1520–1660)', in D. Baker (ed.), *Reform and Reformation: England and the Continent c.1500–c.1750* (1979), pp. 103–31.

J. A. Hilton, 'Catholicism in Elizabethan Northumberland', *Northern History* 13 (1977), pp. 44–58.

J. A. Hilton, 'The Cumbrian Catholics', *Northern History* 16 (1980), pp. 40–58.

P. Lake, 'Puritan identities', *Journal of Ecclesiastical History* 35 (1984), pp. 112–23.

P. Lake, 'Calvinism and the English Church 1570–1635', *Past and Present* 114 (Feb. 1987), pp. 32–76.

D. MacCulloch, 'Catholic and Puritan in Elizabethan Suffolk: a county community polarises', in *Archiv für Reformationsgeschichte* 72 (1981), pp. 232–89.

P. McGrath, 'Elizabethan Catholicism: a Reconsideration', *Journal of Ecclesiastical History* 35 (1984), pp. 414–28.

*J. C. McLelland, 'Calvinism perfecting Thomism? Peter Martyr Vermigli's Question', *Scottish Journal of Theology* 31 (1978), pp. 571–8.

R. B. Manning, 'The Crisis of Episcopal Authority during the Reign of Elizabeth I', *Journal of British Studies* 11 (November 1971), pp. 1–25.

C. Marsh, '"A Graceless and Audacious Companie": The Family of Love in the Parish of Balsham, 1550–1630', in W. J. Sheils and D. Wood (eds), *Voluntary Religion* (Studies in Church History 23 (1986)), pp. 191–208.

J. W. Martin, 'The First that made Separation from the Reformed Church of England', *Archiv für Reformationsgeschichte* 77 (1986), pp. 281–312.

J. W. Martin, 'The Elizabethan Familists', *Baptist Quarterly*, 29 (1982), pp. 267–81.

G. J. Mayhew, 'The Progress of the Reformation in East Sussex 1530–1559: the evidence from wills', *Southern History* 5 (1983), pp. 38–67.

J. Møller, 'The Beginnings of Puritan Covenant Theology', *Journal of Ecclesiastical History* 14 (1963), pp. 46–67.

R. G. Pogson, 'Reginald Pole and the Priorities of Government in Mary Tudor's Church', *Historical Journal* 18 (1975), pp. 3–20.

K. G. Powell, 'The Social Background to the Reformation in Gloucestershire', *Transactions of the Bristol and Gloucestershire Archaeological Society* (1971), pp. 141–57.

B. R. White, 'The English Separatists and John Smyt[h] *Baptist Quarterly* 30 (1984), pp. 344–7: *response to C[...] above.*

P. White, 'The Rise of Arminianism Reconsidered', *Pas[t and Present]* 101 (November 1983), pp. 34–54.

R. Whiting, 'Prayers for the Dead in the Tudor S[...] *Southern History* 5 (1983), pp. 66–94.

M. Zell, 'The Personnel of the Clergy in Kent, in the R[...] Period', *English Historical Review* 89 (1974), pp. 513–[...]

M. Zell, 'The Use of Religious Preambles as a Measure [of] Belief in the Sixteenth Century', *Bulletin of the Institut[...] al Research* 50 (1977), pp. 246–9.

DISSERTATIONS

E. J. Bourgeois II, 'A Ruling Elite: the Governmen[t ...] bridgeshire, circa 1524–88', Cambridge University Ph[...]

D. J. Peet, 'The Mid-Sixteenth Century Parish Clergy, w[...] lar consideration of the dioceses of Norwich and Y[...] bridge University Ph.D., 1980.

R. Whiting, 'The Reformation in the South West o[f ...] Exeter University Ph.D., 1977.

Index

Canterbury, 11, 13–18, 20, 22, 39–40, 43, 68–70, 99, 135, 157
credal predestinarianism, *see* election
creeds, classical Christian, 73
Cressy, David, 18
Cromwell, Thomas, Earl of Essex, 110
Crowley, Robert, 87
Cumbria, 132, 138, 149
Curteys, Richard, Bishop of Chichester, 48

Davenport, Humphrey, 58
Davis, J. F., 68
deacons, 72–3, 115
deans of cathedrals, 120
Dedham *classis*, 50, 165
del Corro, *see* Corro
Delumeau, Jean, 163
Dent, C. M., 72, 78, 96
Devon, 14
Devereux, Robert, Earl of Essex, 60
Devon, 132
Dickens, A. G., 126
dioceses, 101–7, 114
doctors, in Calvinism, 72–3
doctrinal statements, *see* creeds, 39 Articles, 42 Articles
Douai College, 145–6
Dove, John, 178
Dudley, Ambrose, Earl of Warwick, 57
Dudley, John, Duke of Northumberland, 11, 14–20, 83
Dudley, Robert, Earl of Leicester, 52, 95, 176
  and Netherlands, 45–7, 53, 78
  as Puritan patron, 34, 45–6, 56, 60
Durham, bishops of, *see* Barnes
  diocese of, 18

ecclesiology, 72, 77, 97–9
  see also jure divino episcopacy, Presbyterianism
East Anglia, 19, 97, 126–8, 132, 134, 148–9, 156, 158
Eccleshall Castle, 104
edification, 85–7, 90, 92, 98

education, 113, 115
  see also schools, universities
Edward VI, King of England, 1, 11, 14, 19
  Reformation under, 11–19, 24, 31–2, 43, 69–71, 76, 196, 112–13, 129, 131–4, 138, 155–7, 161
elders, in Calvinism, 72
election, doctrine of, 74, 77, 80, 88–93, 97, 156–7
Elizabeth I, Queen of England, 8, 27–61, 71, 74–5, 79, 89, 110, 151, 156
  accession day, 48, 136–7
  assassination attempts on, 53, 152
  deposed by *Regnans in Excelsis*, 46, 145
  forbids prophesyings, 41–3
  and marriage, 37, 45, 47
  obstructs Church reform, 32–3, 39–40, 52, 54, 117–18
  and Reformation under, 19, 23–4, 27–61, 105–8, 113, 133, 135–43, 147, 153–62
  religious views, 28–9, 31–3, 71, 76
Elizabethan Settlement of Religion, 6–7, 27–34, 71, 75, 83, 100, 112, 140, 144, 146, 148, 153, 170–2
Ely, 120
  bishops of, *see* Cox
  diocese, 105–7, 114
Erasmus, Desiderius, 66, 69, 130
Essex, 23, 51, 104, 156, 165, 169
  Earls of, *see* Cromwell, Devereux
eucharist (holy communion), 12–13, 30, 33, 67–8, 72–3, 75, 94, 98, 139, 159, 170
ex officio oath, 50
exchanges of church lands, 105
excommunication, 109
exercises of preaching, 41
exorcism, 118, 167–8
experimental predestinarianism, *see* election

fall of humanity, 74, 90
  see also salvation
Family of Love, 155–7

199

Index

Pole, Reginald, Cardinal
Archbishop of Canterbury,
21–6, 67, 115
Popes, *see* Antichrist, Gregory XIII,
Julius III, Paul IV, Pius V,
papal supremacy, Rome,
bishops of
Porter, H. C., 76
Prayer Book, *see* Book of Common
Prayer
preaching, 3, 6, 13, 23, 41, 67, 71,
86–7, 93, 98, 100, 106, 113–14,
117–18, 120, 137, 139–40, 158
see also exercises, prophesyings,
lectures
predestination, *see* election
Presbyterianism, 38, 40–1, 49–61,
72–4, 76, 84, 87, 93, 97
see also Calvinism, Classical
Movement
Price, F. D., 109
priesthood, *see* clergy
printing, 23, 51
Privy Council, 16, 22, 29, 34, 37, 39,
45–6, 49, 53
propaganda, 23–4
prophesyings, 41–2, 116–18
see also exercises of preaching
Protestantism, character of, 5–6
Protestants, *see* Marian exiles,
martyrs
proto-Arminianism, *see*
Arminianism
purgatory, 1–2, 5–6, 134
Puritanism, character of, 35, 78, 80,
171
Puritans, 40, 47–61, 75, 78, 80,
82–93, 98–100, 104, 115–17,
119, 136, 139, 142, 150, 165,
171–2
and didactic names, 159
and church courts, 107–9
and Leicester, 34, 46
moderate, 54, 59–61, 77, 158
and parliamentary elections, 51–
4, 59
and radicals, 156–62

radical Protestants, *see* Anabaptists,
sectaries, separatists
Ramus, Peter, 80

real presence, *see* eucharist
reason in theology, 94–5, 97–100
rebellions, 7, 14, 21, 25, 47, 60, 129,
132–3, 136, 145
recusancy, Catholic, 23, 106, 110,
145–52
and Arminianism, 96–7
beginning of, 37 (*see also* Roman
Catholics)
Protestant, *see* separatism
Reformatio Legum, 17, 39, 171
Regnans in Excelsis, papal bull, 46,
145
regular clergy, *see* monasteries
Renard, Simon, 20
requiem masses, 1
Revelation, Book of, 79–80
revisionist debate, 80, 125–9, 140–
1, 147–50
Reynolds, John, 78
Ridley, Nicholas, Bishop of
London, 16, 18, 24, 31, 83, 157
Rogationtide processions, 136
Roman Catholics, 40, 48, 78–80,
126, 135, 144–52, 167–8
exiles, 115, 145–50, 152
persecution of, 47, 59, 151–2 (*see
also* recusants)
Rome, bishops of (popes), 4–5, 35–
6, 79–80, 98, 132, 148
see also Western Church
rood screens, 4, 132
rural deaneries, 104, 107
Russell, Francis, Earl of Bedford,
52

sabbatarianism, 66, 139–40
Sackville, Thomas, Lord
Buckhurst, 46
sacraments, 1, 12, 72–3, 75, 92–4,
96, 98, 100, 167
see also baptism, confirmation,
eucharist
St Albans, archdeaconry of, 107
St Asaph, bishops of, *see* Morgan
St Bartholomew massacres (1572),
40
saints, 4, 68, 134
Salisbury, bishops of, *see* Jewel
salvation, 2, 5–6, 60–1, 73–7, 86,
88–93, 98, 156